THE GUIDE FOR CURIOUS MINDS

WORLD CULTURES EXPLAINED

DANIEL SMITH

ROSEN
PUBLISHING®

New York

This edition published in 2015 by:
The Rosen Publishing Group, Inc.
29 East 21st Street
New York, NY 10010

Additional end matter copyright © 2015 by The Rosen Publishing Group, Inc.

Library of Congress Cataloging-in-Publication Data

Smith, Daniel, 1976–
World cultures explained/Daniel Smith.—First Edition.
    pages cm.—(The guide for curious minds)
Includes bibliographical references and index.
ISBN 978-1-4777-8130-2 (library bound)
1. Ethnology—Juvenile literature. 2. Cross-cultural studies—Juvenile literature. 3. Comparative civilization—Juvenile literature. I. Title.
GN333.S65 2015
306—dc23

3 1350 00348 4468

2014024525

Manufactured in the United States of America

© 2015 ELWIN STREET PRODUCTIONS www.elwinstreet.com

Contents

GEOGRAPHY

The world as we know it

What is a country?

A country is a defined geographical area which is usually controlled by an independent government. The government, of whatever sort, makes laws, and is responsible for general administration, law and order, national defence, the economy and taxation; most governments also take a role in other aspects of life like education, transportation, social protection, agriculture, natural resources and cultural affairs.

Throughout this book the word "country" is used to mean a sovereign nation – that is to say, an internationally recognised territory and its people under the authority of a government. By this definition there are 195 countries in 2014, with Russia being the largest in terms of area (at over 17 million square kilometres or 6.6 million square miles) and Vatican City being the smallest (less than half a square kilometre or one fifth of a square mile). Every country is a member of the United Nations, with the exception of Vatican City, who hasn't chosen to be part of the organization, and Taiwan and Kosovo, which have not gained the complete international recognition that would allow them to become members of the UN. For a full list of countries, see pages 61–72.

Nationhood

The words "country" and "nation" are often used interchangeably but nationhood is a more fluid concept. Sometimes a nation is defined as any community of people with a shared identity. This identity might include shared history, behavioural patterns, language, religion, culture and ethnic origins. For a closer look at nationality, see Chapter 3.

The first country

The earliest known civilisation was the Sumerian, which included roughly 12 city-states in Mesopotamia (modern day Iraq). However, these city-states were not independent and shared control of the Sumerian civilisation until they were unified by Sargon of Akkad (a.k.a. Agade) around 2300 BCE. By then Pharaoh Menes had unified Upper and Lower Egypt (c.3100–2850 BCE), and so Egypt is generally thought of as the first country in the sense of having political unity and a national identity. San Marino, founded in 301 CE, is usually regarded as the world's oldest national republic.

What is a continent?

When geographers, historians or politicians are dealing with large areas of the world they will often talk about the continents, which are great continuous landmasses usually made up of several countries. There are various continental models of the world, but the seven-continent model is the most common and comprises Africa, Antarctica, Asia, Europe, North America, Oceania and South America.

Though we might not feel it, these continents are on the move. For instance, every year South America and Africa are moving about 7 cm (3 inches) apart. Alfred Wegener, a German astronomer, first put forward the theory of "continental drift" in 1912. He and several other scientists had noticed that different continents had shapes which seemed to go together. If you look at a map you can see how South America used to sit roughly where the Niger Delta is now. While humans may control national borders, nature is definitely in control of the continents.

PERMIAN 255 million years ago

TRIASSIC 200 million years ago

JURASSIC 135 million years ago

CRETACEOUS 65 million years ago

ABOVE Continental drift, caused by the shifting of their underlying "tectonic plates."

World map (physical)

Maps of the world tend to be either "political," showing territorial borders of countries, or "physical," showing geographic features, such as mountains, soil type or land use. Some physical maps are extended to geological maps, which show not only the physical surface, but such things as the characteristics of the underlying rock, fault lines and subsurface structures.

ABOVE A "Robinson projection" world map (see page 15 on projections).

This physical world map shows details of terrain and type of land – the rich green areas denote farmland, pasture, forest and jungle, while the paler white, yellow and red areas denote a lack of greenery, such as deserts and ice caps. The blue area is, of course, water – the oceans, sea, lakes and rivers – and the darker areas of water denote the deeper channels and parts of the oceans.

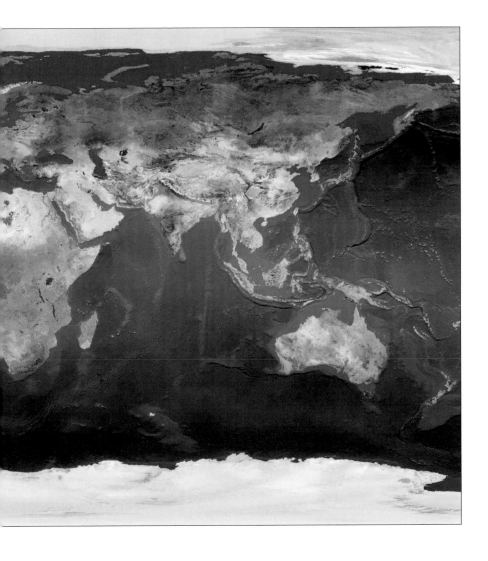

Largest and smallest countries

The following tables show the world's largest and smallest countries, ranked by total area, together with the total lengths of their boundaries. Some countries have a far greater proportion of inland water included in their total area than others. India (10 per cent) and Canada (9 per cent) have far more inland water than any other large country, while none of the smallest countries contains any significant body of water at all.

Though Russia still remains the largest country on Earth, the former Soviet Union was even larger, covering about 22 million km² (8.5 million square miles), 15 per cent of the world's land surface.

Ten largest countries

Largest ten	Total area	Total boundary
Russia	17,075,200 Km² 6,592,735 sq miles	57,670 km 22,266 miles
Canada	9,984,670 Km² 3,855,081 sq miles	210,973 km 81,457 miles
United States	9,631,418 Km² 3,718,690 sq miles	31,958 km 12,339 miles
China	9,596,960 Km² 3,705,386 sq miles	36,617 km 14,138 miles
Brazil	8,511,965 Km² 3,286,470 sq miles	22,182 km 8,564 miles
Australia	7,686,850 Km² 2,967,893 sq miles	25,760 km 9,946 miles
India	3,287,263 Km² 1,269,212 sq miles	11,968 km 7,437 miles
Argentina	2,780,400 Km² 1,073,512 sq miles	13,888 km 8,630 miles
Kazakhstan	2,717,300 Km² 1,049,150 sq miles	12,012 km 4,638 miles
Algeria	2,381,740 Km² 919,590 sq miles	7,341 km 2,834 miles

FACT
Russia is almost twice as large as the second–largest country in the world, Canada. It stretches across two continents, from Scandinavia and central Europe in the west to the shores of northern Asia in the east. However, much of this land is made up of cold and barren plains, known as *steppe*, and very few people live in these areas. Taken as an average temperature across the nation, Russia is the coldest country on Earth.

Ten smallest countries

Smallest ten	Total area	Total boundary
Malta	316 km² 122 sq miles	197 km 76 miles
Maldives	300 km² 116 sq miles	644 km 249 miles
Saint Kitts & Nevis	261 km² 101 sq miles	135 km 52 miles
Marshall Islands	181 km² 70 sq miles	370 km 143 miles
Liechtenstein	160 km² 62 sq miles	76 km 29 miles
San Marino	61 km² 24 sq miles	39 km 15 miles
Tuvalu	26 km² 10 sq miles	24 km 9 miles
Nauru	21 km² 8 sq miles	30 km 12 miles
Monaco	2 km² 0.75 sq miles	8.5 km 3.3 miles
Vatican City	0.44 km² 0.17 sq miles	3.2 km 1.2 miles

Land boundaries

As is to be expected, the countries with the largest areas tend to be those with the longest boundaries, but there are some exceptions – China is only the fourth largest country by area but has the longest land boundary while Australia, the sixth largest country, has no land boundaries at all. While two of the four largest countries have the equal-greatest number of neighbours (China and Russia officially have 14 each), Canada, the second largest country, has only one neighbour, and the United States, the third largest, has only two.

Borders and border disputes

There is significant variation around the world in how easy or difficult it is to pass through borders between countries. For example, many of the borders between member states of the European Union are completely uncontrolled, while disputed borders such as those between Israel and the Palestinian Territories are heavily patrolled.

At any one time there are many disputes over the control of land between two or more countries. Such disputes can lead to war or terrorism, but others rumble on unresolved but peaceful for years. Occasionally, the International Court of Justice gets involved and sometimes two countries will agree to a "line of control," which acts as a *de facto* border but does not have international legitimacy.

Among the bloodiest border disputes of recent times is that between India and Pakistan, who have gone to war over the border region of Kashmir several times since 1947. The Golan Heights has been a source of tension between Syria and Israel since Israel claimed control of the area after the Six Day War of 1967; it is still administered and controlled by Israel, though it is neither claimed nor recognised as Israeli territory. Elsewhere, Turkey and Greece have argued over who rules where in Cyprus since control of the island was divided in 1974. And in Africa, international arbitration has done little to improve relations between Ethiopia and Eritrea over the ownership of Badme.

Coastlines

The country with the longest coastline is Canada, whose total shoreline is almost five times as long as the Equator. Island groups by their nature have disproportionately long coastlines – the Philippines have the fourth-longest coastline of any country despite being 71st in terms of area.

Around one fifth of the world's population lives within 32 km (20 miles) of a shoreline. In Australia, 85 per cent of the population lives within 48 km (30 miles) of the coast (99 per cent in Tasmania)

ABOVE Coastal erosion destroyed this house in Denmark.

FACT

At 122 km² (47 square miles), Disney World in Florida is bigger than the world's five smallest countries.

FACT

Tuvalu, a Pacific nation made up of nine atolls, is particularly at risk if sea levels rise as much as some experts predict it will in the years to come. With its coastline already receding and with a high point only 4.6 m (15 feet) above sea level, the government of Tuvalu has asked New Zealand about the possibility of re-housing its 11,000 residents.

and 11 of the world's 15 largest cities lie along the coast or on estuaries. But with sea levels rising as global warming takes hold, coastal erosion is becoming a major problem. Over 70 per cent of the world's sandy beaches are already retreating. The Intergovernmental Panel on Climate Change predicts that sea levels will rise by up to 1 metre (40 inches) during the twenty-first century. Some environmental scientists estimate that every millimetre rise equates to 1.5 metres of shoreline erosion, so that a 1-metre (40-inch) rise could cause coastlines to retreat by almost 1,500 metres (1 mile) – with serious social, environmental and economic consequences.

Coastal management (or coastal defence) is humankind's main weapon against coastal erosion. Coastal management can either involve "hard" engineering, like building sea walls, or "soft" engineering. "Soft" engineering methods include strengthening a beach with imported sand, building and maintaining sand dunes, draining excess water using a pumping station or allowing land to erode and naturally stabilise.

FACT

Gerardus Mercator is credited with first using the term "atlas" for a collection of maps. He chose the term atlas in honor of the Titan King of Mauritania, a renowned philosopher, mathematician and astronomer.

World maps and map projections

A map is a two-dimensional representation of a three-dimensional world, so it will inevitably distort some features. Therefore, cartographers must decide what combination of geographical features to focus on. These may include area, bearing, direction, distance, scale and shape. How they choose to represent these features on a flat surface is known as a map projection.

Among the most famous map projections is the one Gerardus Mercator created in 1569. He used a rectangular-shaped map with lines of longitude and latitude represented as parallel lines at right angles to each other. This means that his projection is more accurate close to the equator and becomes less accurate nearer to the poles, where landmasses appear much larger than they really are. Mercator's model remained popular well into the twentieth century.

Another of the most commonly-used projections today is one developed by Arthur Robinson in the 1960s (see pp.8-9). Robinson used an elliptical shape, flattened at the top and bottom; its curved meridians give the impression of the Earth's spherical nature. Unfortunately, it does partly distort area, distance, scale and shape.

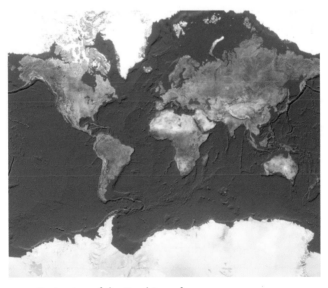

ABOVE Mercator Projection of the Earth's surface.

Time zones

In primitive times the only important indicators of time were natural ones: sunrise, midday and sunset. The invention of mechanical clocks allowed the day to be divided into uniform segments but communities still used local time, based on the Sun being highest in the sky at midday at their meridian of longitude. This meant that cities in the west of a country could be minutes or hours ahead of those in the east. With the coming of the railways, most countries saw the need to standardise clocks throughout the nation, usually based on midday at the meridian of the capital.

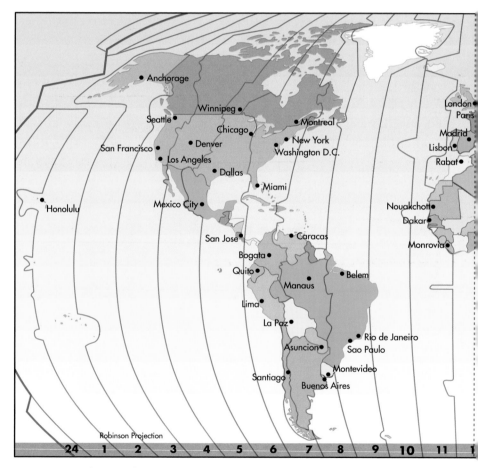

ABOVE Map showing how time zones across the world differ from GMT.

By the late nineteenth century, navigators and governments saw the need for a single prime meridian and for universal time for the world. As a result, the International Meridian Conference met in Washington, DC in October 1884 and decided to adopt the Greenwich Meridian as the Prime Meridian and Greenwich Mean Time (GMT) as universal time.

Some enthusiasts hoped that GMT would be used throughout the world for all purposes, with a single time in all locations. However, this was clearly not practical, so a time–zone system was devised, based on GMT, by which (with a few exceptions) it would be the same minute in all places, but the hour would differ.

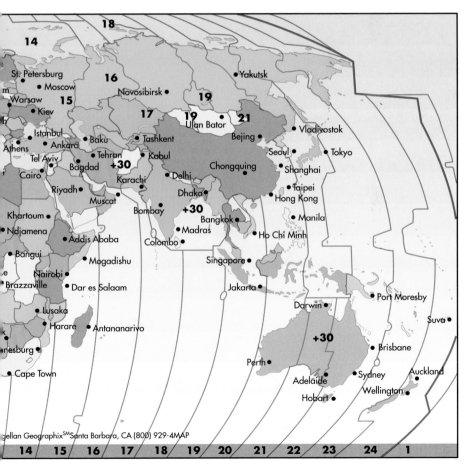

Landlocked countries

42 countries are "landlocked," having no coastline of their own. Traditionally, being landlocked has been regarded as a disadvantage because these countries have no direct access to fishing or seaborne trade. Coastal regions have tended to be more prosperous and heavily populated than inland zones. The United Nations Convention on the Law of the Sea says that a landlocked country must have right of access to and from the sea, without taxation of traffic through intervening states.

ABOVE The mountainous, double landlocked nation of Liechtenstein.

FACT

There are two "double landlocked" countries – that is, countries whose neighbours are also landlocked. These are Liechtenstein (bordered by Switzerland and Austria) and Uzbekistan (bordered by Kazakhstan, Turkmenistan, Afghanistan, Tajikistan and Kyrgyzstan).

Island states

There are 39 countries that are islands and have no land boundaries with other countries. Island nations include Antigua and Barbuda, Australia, the Bahamas, Bahrain, Cuba, Cyprus, Iceland, Jamaica, Japan, Madagascar, Mauritius, New Zealand, Philippines, Saint Lucia, Saint Vincent and the Grenadines, Samoa, São Tomé and Principe, Seychelles, Singapore and Sri Lanka.

Major landlocked countries around the world

Landlocked country	Neighbouring countries
Afghanistan	Turkmenistan, Uzbekistan, Tajikistan, China, Pakistan and Iran
Austria	Germany, the Czech Republic, Slovakia, Hungary, Slovenia, Italy, Switzerland and Liechtenstein
Belarus	Poland, Latvia, Lithuania, Russia and Ukraine
Bhutan	India and China
Bolivia	Brazil, Paraguay, Argentina, Chile and Peru
Botswana	Namibia, Zambia, Zimbabwe and South Africa
Chad	Cameroon, Nigeria, Niger, Libya, Sudan and the Central African Republic
Czech Republic	Germany, Poland, Slovakia and Austria
Ethiopia	Eritrea, Djibouti, Somalia, Kenya and Sudan
Kazakhstan	Russia, China, Uzbekistan, Kyrgyzstan and Turkmenistan
Laos	China, Vietnam, Cambodia, Thailand and Myanmar
Luxembourg	Belgium, France and Germany
Mongolia	Russia and China
Nepal	China and India
Niger	Algeria, Libya, Chad, Nigeria, Benin, Burkina Faso and Mali
Switzerland	France, Germany, Austria and Italy
Uganda	Sudan, Kenya, Tanzania, Rwanda and the Democratic Republic of the Congo
Zimbabwe	Zambia, Mozambique, South Africa, Botswana and Namibia

Land use

The diagram below shows how much of the planet's land is used for agriculture, how much is forest and how much is barren or has been urbanised.

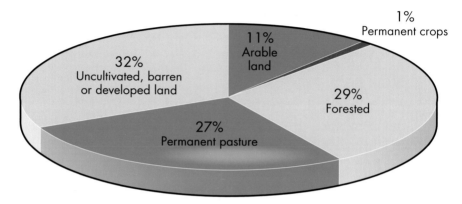

The five countries with the most forest cover are Suriname (90.5 per cent), Solomon Islands (88.8 per cent), Gabon (84.7 per cent), the Bahamas (84.1 per cent) and Brunei (83.9 per cent). Oman has no forest cover at all. In general, however, we live in a world of metropolises; just 1.5 per cent of the Earth's surface is home to 49.2 per cent of the global population, who live in urban areas. The table below shows the most and least urbanised countries in 2005.

Highest and lowest urban populations in the world

Urban Population	%	Urban Population	%
World	49.2		
Top Five		Bottom Five	
Monaco	100.0	Papua New Guinea	13.2
Singapore	100.0	Uganda	12.4
Vatican City	100.0	Burundi	10.6
Belgium	97.3	East Timor	7.8
Kuwait	96.4	Bhutan	7.7

Seas and oceans

Seas and oceans cover 71 per cent of the Earth's surface. There are five oceans (the Arctic, the Atlantic, the Indian, the Pacific and the Southern) and dozens of seas. A sea is defined as a body of salt water that is partially or fully enclosed by land.

Oceans by size

Ocean	sq miles	sq km
Pacific	60,060,000	155,557,000
Atlantic	29,637,900	76,762,000
Indian	26,469,470	68,556,000
Southern	7,848,250	20,327,000
Arctic	5,427,020	14,056,000

The five largest seas in the world

Sea	sq miles	sq km
Coral Sea	1,850,200	4,791,000
Arabian Sea	1,492,000	3,863,000
South China Sea	1,423,000	3,685,000
Mediterranean Sea	971,000	2,516,000
Caribbean Sea	971,000	2,516,000

FACT

The Southern Ocean only officially became an ocean when it was approved by the International Hydrographic Organization in 2000.

ABOVE The Barrier Reef of Belize, in the Caribbean Sea.

Oceanic features

Ocean trenches are topographic depressions that form the deepest parts of the ocean floor. Trenches form where tectonic plate boundaries come together. The deepest known ocean trench is the Mariana Trench (or Marianas Trench), situated in the western part of the North Pacific Ocean at a depth of 10,911 m (35,798 feet). The next deepest are Mindanao Deep (or Philippine Trench), Kuril-Kamchatka Trench, Tonga Trench and Japan Trench, all of which go to a depth in excess of 9,000 m (30,000 feet).

FACT

The Great Barrier Reef is not a single living organism but rather a system of about 900 islands and over 3,000 coral reefs. In 2004, the Great Barrier Reef Marine Park became the largest protected sea area in the world.

There are several types of biotic reefs in the sea but the largest are coral reefs. A coral reef is a large, biogenic limestone formation that gathers around the reef inhabitants as skeletal material. Over time this material and other debris knit together as the life-forms attached to the reef develop. The largest and most famous example of a coral reef is the Great Barrier Reef, which lies off the coast of Queensland in northeastern Australia. The next largest is the Barrier Reef of Belize.

Maritime claims

Most countries stake a claim over the sea off their coasts, if they have them. The extent of these claims is governed by the United Nations Convention on the Law of the Sea (UNCLOS), which says that economic or fishing zones cannot extend beyond 200 nautical miles (nm). Not all nations claim the full limit, and often the proximity of neighbouring states prevents countries from using the full 200 nm. Here are the standard claims open to a country:

UNCLOS maritime claims	Description	Limit
Territorial sea	The sovereignty of a coastal state extends to an adjacent belt of sea, the air space over it and the seabed and subsoil under it.	12 nm
Contiguous zone	A zone over which a country may exercise certain customs, immigration and sanitary controls to prevent infringement within its territory or territorial sea.	24 nm
Exclusive economic zone	A zone in which a country has the exclusive right to: research and explore; exploit, conserve and manage natural resources; exercise jurisdiction over the establishment and use of artificial islands, installations and structures. Some countries, including the UK, instead exercise a right to an exclusive fishing zone.	200 nm
Continental shelf	The seabed and subsoil of the submarine areas that extend beyond a country's territorial sea.	350 nm*

* Maritime claims over the seabed can be claimed to a distance of either 350 nautical miles from the coast, or 100 nautical miles beyond the point where the depth of the ocean reaches 2,500 metres (8,202 feet).

Environmental geography

Environmental geography looks to understand the relationship between humans and the environment, especially the impact of human activities on the natural world. Some of the major disciplines involved in environmental geography are outlined below.

Biogeography *tracks, predicts and tries to understand the reasons for distribution patterns of different species. Important factors include climate variation, continental drift, energy sources, extinction, geographic constraints and speciation.*

Geology *looks at the Earth as a whole, and especially its physical properties and how it has evolved. Geology has been key to answering some of the Big Questions, like how old the Earth is (around 4.6 billion years), and is also vital to managing natural resources.*

Geomorphology *studies landforms, including how they originated and evolved. It is used in predicting future developments, such as landslides, and can assist in projects such as river and coastal protection.*

Hydrology *is the study of water throughout the world, including its movement, distribution and quality. It is an essential part of achieving sensible water resource management.*

Meteorology *is the study of the atmosphere, especially weather processes and forecasting. Through the tracking of features such as temperature, pressure and water vapour, meteorologists attempt to understand weather events.*

Environmental geography also tries to understand how humans conceptualise their environment. For instance, a human view of the world might be influenced by social, industrial, economic or technological factors – considerations which have a huge influence on mankind's relationship with the planet.

Human impact on the environment

Some of the planet's greatest problems are ongoing environmental issues, especially petrochemical pollution and deforestation, which together are thought to be contributing to climate change. The Environmental Performance Index was devised by environmentalists at Yale and Columbia Universities and takes into account 20 factors, including pollution levels, natural resources and environmental management strategies. It ranks 178 different nations. In 2014, the five countries awarded the highest ratings were Switzerland, Luxembourg, Australia, Singapore, and Czech Republic. The five countries with the lowest scores were Somalia, Mali, Haiti, Lesotho, and Afghanistan.

Climate change

The global climate naturally varies over time, but global warming is a particular cause of concern to the world. Potential effects of global warming are rising sea levels, ozone layer depletion, extreme weather events and weakened agriculture. One of the key causes of global warming is the emission of "greenhouse gases" (such as carbon dioxide and methane), which trap and radiate heat. Below are the countries with the biggest carbon dioxide emissions in 2013:

Country	% of total
World Total	100 %
China	22.95 %
United States	15.5 %
India	5.14 %
Russia	4.9 %
Brazil	4.12 %
Japan	3.54 %
Indonesia	2.3 %
Germany	2.23 %

Pollution

The more we consume as a planet, the more waste we produce and so pollution becomes an ever-growing problem. There are many different types of pollution – air, water, radioactive and even noise and light – which have negative effects on the environment, human health and quality of life. The countries with the highest air pollution emissions are the United States, Russia, China and Japan.

FACT

The Kyoto Protocol is a 1997 proposal committing all signatories to reduce emissions of carbon dioxide and five other greenhouse gases that went into effect on February 16, 2005. As of 2014, 191 nations have ratified the agreement, but notable exceptions include Canada, which withdrew in 2011, and the United States.

Deforestation

Deforestation is the destruction of forested areas. Though rainforests only cover about 6 per cent of the Earth's land surface, they account for 80 per cent of all land vegetation, a third of all plant matter and are home to important and rare animal species. Forests are often removed to make way for agricultural projects, urban development or simply to take economic advantage of the valuable forest resources. As well as destroying the habitat of all kinds of flora and fauna, deforestation has a negative effect on the water cycle and global warming.

Protected areas

A protected area is a piece of land or sea that is especially dedicated to the protection and maintenance of biological diversity, and protected as such under law. Columbia and Venezuela have almost three quarters of their land protected, while Saudi Arabia, Zambia and Tanzania all have around 40 per cent protected, and Germany and Austria both protect over 30 per cent.

UNESCO World Heritage Sites

The United Nations Educational, Scientific and Cultural Organisation (UNESCO) operates the World Heritage List to help protect and preserve sites of outstanding cultural or natural importance. The list grew out of the UN's 1972 convention *Concerning the Protection of World Cultural and Natural Heritage.*

As of 2014 there were 1,007 sites listed in 161 countries. Of these, 779 were cultural sites, 197 were natural sites and 31 were mixed. Italy (50) has the most sites listed, followed by China (47), Spain (44), Germany (39), France (39), Mexico (32) and India (32).

ABOVE The Shinto Itsukushima Shrine in Miyajima, Japan is a UNESCO World Heritage site.

FACT
The Galapagos Islands was one of the first areas to go on the heritage list, back in 1978. The archipelago is under the jurisdiction of Ecuador, and its extraordinary array of flora and fauna led Charles Darwin to some of his greatest insights on natural selection and evolution.

Heritage in Danger

UNESCO also lists 46 sites as World Heritage in Danger, designed to inform the international community of threats to a listed site and encourage action to protect it. These threats might include war, natural disaster, pollution, poaching, urbanisation or tourist development. Countries with sites on the list include Afghanistan, Belize, Bolivia, Chile, Democratic Republic of the Congo, Egypt, Ethiopia, Georgia, Honduras, Indonesia, Iraq, Jerusalem (site proposed by Jordan), Madagascar, Mali, Niger, Panama, Peru, the United States and Venezuela.

Destruction and regeneration

An example of UNESCO's work in protecting and renewing cultural heritage can be seen in the town of Mostar, spanning the Neretva River in Bosnia and Herzegovina. Mostar rose to prominence in the fifteenth and sixteenth centuries and was symbolised by its Old Bridge (or *Stari Most*, which gave the town its name). The bridge was virtually destroyed in 1990 during Yugoslavia's civil war, but the area was added to the world heritage list in 2005, thus becoming a focus for restoration. With the help of UNESCO, the bridge and surrounding Old Town were rebuilt and have become symbols of cooperation between the country's different ethnic and religious groups.

Unfortunately, heritage listing could do nothing to protect Afghanistan's Buddhas of Bamiyan. In 2001, the Taliban regime oversaw the destruction of the two huge Buddhas, which were carved into a cliff face in the Bamiyan Valley. The figures dated back to the fifth or sixth century and were the largest standing Buddhas in the world. The Taliban considered them idolatrous and blew them up, causing international outrage. Japan is now leading a movement to have the statues rebuilt with the help of UNESCO.

PEOPLE

Population

The world's population is growing at a phenomenal rate. There are over 7.2 billion people in our world and that number is growing by around 80 million people per year. The global population reached 1 billion around 1800 and took 130 years to reach 2 billion around 1930. Since then we have been multiplying ever more quickly – it only took us 12 years to grow from 5 billion (reached in 1987) to 6 billion (reached in 1999).

Demography is the scientific study of population statistics including birth rates, death rates, migration and aging. By studying demography, we get a better understanding of how societies are structured and how they might function in the future. The first modern census was taken in Britain in 1801.

ABOVE China has at least six cities with populations over 5 million, including Hong Kong, where the population of the metropolitan area is estimated to be over 7 million.

Ten most populous countries in the world 2013

Country	Total population
World	7,162,119,434
China	1,393,783,836
India	1,267,401,849
United States	322,583,006
Indonesia	252,812,245
Brazil	202,033,670
Pakistan	185,132,926
Nigeria	178,516,904
Bangladesh	158,512,570
Russia	142,467,651
Japan	126,999,808

Unpopulous countries

At the other end of the scale from China and India, there are several countries in the world that have a total population of less than 100,000. Many of these are small island nations such as Antigua and Barbuda, Marshall Islands, Palau and Nauru, though there are also some European micro-countries, the smallest of which are Liechtenstein, Monaco and San Marino. The world's least populous country is also the smallest: Vatican City, with a population recently counted at 800.

FACT

The United Nations forecasts that India's population will overtake that of China by 2050 and that their joint populations will account for over half of the total world population.

Population density

Population density tells us the average number of people per square kilometre in a given area. When the populations of the nations of the world are considered in comparison to those nations" land areas, the most densely populated turn out to be small "city-states' – Monaco, Singapore and Vatican City – though the urbanised island-states of Malta and Maldives are also very dense. While these countries average thousands of people per square kilometre, countries dominated by desert such as Botswana, Australia, Namibia and Mongolia can average as low as 1.5 people per square kilometre.

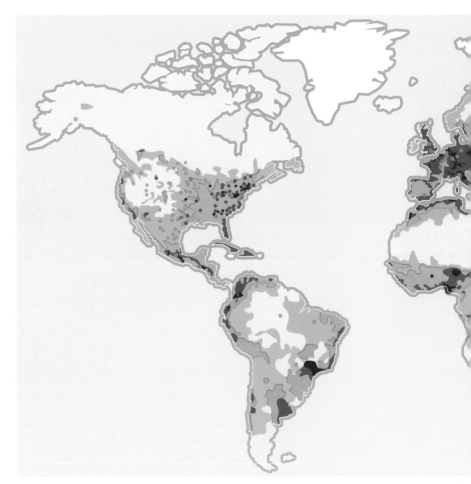

ABOVE World map with indications of population density.

Gender balance and imbalance

In the world as a whole, men and women have a very good chance of finding a partner, since there are about 101 men for every 100 women. However, men in Qatar may have a little more difficulty as they outnumber women by 188 to 100. They might want to go to Estonia, where there are 119 women for every 100 men.

In China, a traditional favoritism towards male children, together with the government's "one child policy," have gradually created a gender imbalance that now stands at 117:100, with males in the majority.

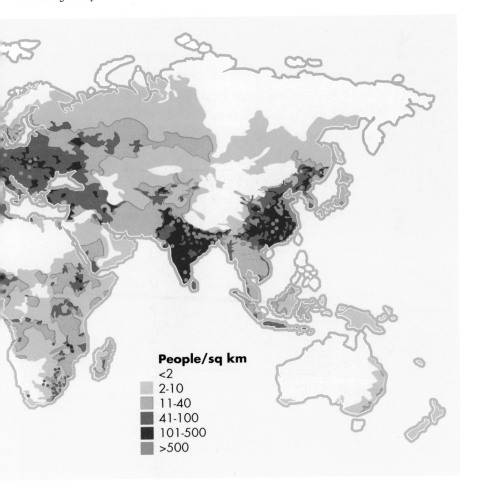

People/sq km
<2
2-10
11-40
41-100
101-500
>500

Urban living

What is a city?

There is no definitive set of rules that says how a town becomes a city, but most cities have a significant level of size, population and importance, and often some legal recognition. Cities usually have a complex infrastructure to meet a variety of needs, including residential, commercial, industrial and administrative. Though urbanisation is a relatively recent development in terms of human history, around 48 per cent of the world's population now live in cities and that figure is expected to rise to 60 per cent by 2030. Virtually all big, developed nations have large urban populations.

In medieval Europe, cities were powerful political units. For instance, trade in northern Europe was dominated for a long time by the Hanseatic League, an alliance of prosperous commercial cities. On the peninsula that would later become Italy, there were several powerful city-states, including Florence, Genoa, Milan and Venice. Sakai achieved similar importance in medieval Japan.

However, it was the dawn of the industrial age that caused the most rapid increase in urbanisation, first in Europe, but soon

ABOVE New York City skyline.

FACT
Many cities claim to be the oldest continuously occupied city in the world, but there is a good chance that the very earliest is in Syria, where the cities of Damascus and Aleppo both have strong claims to the title.

throughout the world. In modern day Africa and Asia, rural communities are moving from the countryside to the cities in a similar way to that experienced in Europe in the nineteenth and twentieth centuries.

Urban geography

Urban geography is the study of cities, their history and their development. Cities are highly complex organisms. While they are able to take advantage of a concentration of people, resources and infrastructure, they also face many difficult problems, from crime and poverty to transport and communications. Urban geography tries to understand and find solutions to these problems.

With a 100 per cent urban population, Singapore ranks as the world's most urbanised nation. Next come Kuwait (98.4 per cent), Belgium (97.4 per cent) and Qatar (95.8 per cent). The least urbanised nation is Burundi (11.0 per cent), followed by Uganda (13.3 per cent) and Sri Lanka (15.1 per cent).

The world's ten largest cities 2014

City	Country	Population (millions)	City	Country	Population (millions)
Tokyo	Japan	38.0	Sao Paulo	Brazil	21
Delhi	India	25	Osaka	Japan	20
Shanghai	China	23	Beijing	China	20
Mexico City	Mexico	21	New York	U.S.A.	18.5
Mumbai	India	21	Cairo	Egypt	18.5

Biggest and fastest growing

There are many ways to count urban populations, as city boundaries often change and an "urban agglomeration" may cover a much larger area than the traditional core of a city. There are 411 cities in the world with populations over one million.

None of the ten largest cities shown on the previous page are among the fastest growing. From 2000 to 2005, Beihai in China expanded by 11.5 per cent, more than anywhere else. India has three of the fastest growing cities in the world, in Ghaziabad (5.2 per cent), Surat (5 per cent) and Faridabad (4.4 per cent). The six other cities making up the ten fastest growing are Sana'a in Yemen (5 per cent), Kabul in Afghanistan (4.7 per cent), Bamako in Mali (4.5 per cent), Lagos in Nigeria (4.4 per cent), Dar es Salaam in Tanzania (4.4 per cent) and Chittagong in Bangladesh (4.3 per cent).

Quality of life

The *Economist* magazine's Intelligence Unit has constructed an urban quality of life index which rates cities on 39 different criteria, including material well-being, health, recreation, crime, community life, climate, job security and political freedom. Highest ranking in recent years were Switzerland's two main cities, Geneva and Zurich, closely followed by Vancouver (Canada), Vienna (Austria), Dusseldorf, Frankfurt and Munich (Germany), as well as Australia and New Zealand's largest respective cities, Sydney and Auckland.

Nice if you can afford it...

Unfortunately, high standards of living – and earning – tend to mean that these "desirable" cities become very expensive to live in. A recent survey by Mercer Human Resource Consulting revealed that both Geneva and Zurich are among the ten most expensive cities on the planet, though not as expensive as Tokyo and Osaka in Japan, which are at the top of the charts. Other exorbitant cities include London (UK), Moscow (Russia), Seoul (South Korea), Copenhagen (Denmark), Hong Kong (China) and Oslo (Norway).

Fertility

The fertility rate is the average number of children that would be born per woman if all women lived to the end of their childbearing years (adjusted for variations in fertility with age). Fertility rates are declining across the world as a whole, but especially in Europe. On the other hand, birth rates are still very high in many developing nations.

FACT
Over 50 per cent of women in sub-Saharan Africa have their first child before the age of 20. The average age for an American woman to give birth for the first time is 25.

World's highest and lowest fertility rates 2014

Country	Fertility rate (births per woman)	Country	Fertility rate (births per woman)
Top five		Bottom five	
Niger	6.89	Singapore	.80
Mali	6.16	Macau	.93
Burundi	6.14	Taiwan	1.11
Somalia	6.08	South Korea	1.25
Uganda	5.97	British Virgin Islands	1.25

FACT
The 10 countries with the highest death rate are South Africa, Ukraine, Lesotho, Chad, Guinea-Bissau, Bulgaria, Afghanistan, Central African Republic, Somalia and Russia.

Migration rate

The biggest reason for migration is economic. That is to say, most people move in the hope of finding employment and financial security. This sort of migration often reflects a lack of opportunity in a migrant's homeland and also particularly favourable circumstances in the destination country, but there are other reasons for migration such as war or political, cultural and religious persecution. The net migration rate of a country is the annual number of immigrants minus the number of emigrants per 1,000 people. A positive figure shows net immigration and a negative number net emigration. Here are the five countries with the highest and lowest levels of each.

Country net migration 2014

Country	Highest net migration (per 1,000 people)	Country	Lowest net migration (per 1,000 people)
Lebanon	83.82	Syria	-113.51
Qatar	27.35	Federated States of Micronesia	-20.93
Zimbabwe	21.78	Tonga	-17.85
British Virgin Islands	17.69	Nauru	-14.12
Jordan	17.22	Maldives	-12.67

Population growth rate

The balance of birth, death and migration rates gives the population growth rate of a country as a whole. There are eight countries with population growth rates of over 3 per cent, the fastest-growing being Afghanistan (4.77 per cent), Yemen (3.45 per cent) and Kuwait (3.44 per cent, largely due to having the third highest rate of net immigration). There are two countries with a zero growth rate (Germany and Botswana) and 19 with negative growth rates, the bottom three being Latvia (-0.69 per cent), Trinidad and Tobago (-0.74 per cent) and Bulgaria (-0.89 per cent).

Health

People in different countries can have hugely different expectations of how long they are likely to live and how healthy they will be. As a general rule, the richer the country, the older and healthier people can hope to become. Two of the best indicators of a nation's general health are the infant mortality rate and life expectancy at birth.

Infant mortality rate and life expectancy

The infant mortality rate is the number of deaths of children under one year old per 1,000 live births per year. In some Scandinavian countries, the advances of modern health and medicine have reduced the infant mortality rate to only 2–3 out of every 1,000 babies born. Meanwhile, a number of countries in sub-Saharan Africa, as well as Afghanistan, still suffer infant mortality well over 100 out of every 1,000, as well as life expectancies that are well below world average.

Highest and lowest life expectancies 2014

Country	Life expectancy (Years)	Country	Life expectancy (Years)
World	70		
Top five		Bottom five	
Monaco	89.57	Chad	49.44
Japan	84.48	South Africa	49.56
Singapore	84.38	Guinea-Bissau	49.87
San Marino	83.18	Afghanistan	50.49
Andorra	82.65	Swaziland	50.54

FACT

The oldest ratified human life was that of Jeanne Calment of France, who died in 1997, aged 122 years and 164 days.

Medical services

Many of us take it for granted that we"ll be able to go and see the doctor up the road if we get ill, but this is not the case for a very great many people in the world. While infant mortality rates and life expectancy are good indicators of the actual health of a nation, the number of doctors and the amount spent on health give a good idea of how seriously a government takes the health of its people.

There are 33 countries with fewer than 10 physicians per 100,000 people. The countries with the fewest doctors are all in Africa: Mozambique, Rwanda and Tanzania all have two doctors among every 100,000 people, while in Mali there is only one. The world average is 149, while some countries have over 500. Though most of these countries are wealthy developed nations, the poorer Caribbean nations of Cuba and Saint Lucia both also manage over 500 doctors per 100,000 inhabitants.

The country which spends the most on health (the United States) spends over 350 times more than the country with the lowest health budget (Democratic Republic of Congo).

Caloric intake

Many people in the developed world eat too much of the wrong foods and have caloric intakes that are so high they cause health problems such as obesity, diabetes, high blood pressure, high cholesterol levels and heart disease. In countries such as the United States, Portugal, Greece and Austria, people on average consume more than 50 per cent above the World Health Organisation recommended intake.

The opposite is true in the developing world, where limited access to nutritious food causes lowered immunity to disease and more obvious problems like malnutrition and starvation. In Eritrea, the average food intake is only 63 per cent of the recommended healthy minimum.

Causes of death

Below is a table showing the leading causes of death in both low-income and high income countries around the world in 2012. The low-income countries suffer high fatality rates from diseases that have been virtually eliminated as causes of death in many high-income countries, like diarrhoeal diseases and tuberculosis. Lack of education and treatment have also allowed HIV/AIDS to exact an enormous toll.

Low-income countries	Deaths in 2012	High-Income countries	Deaths in 2012
Lower respiratory infections	9,100,000	Ischaemic heart disease	158,000,000
HIV/AIDS	6,500,000	Stroke	9,500,000
Diarrhoeal diseases	5,300,000	Trachea/bronchus/lung cancer	4,900,000
Stroke	5,200,000	Alzheimer disease and other dementias	4,200,000
Ischaemic heart disease	3,900,000	Chronic obstructive pulmonary disease	3,100,000
Malaria	3,500,000	Low respiratory infections	3,100,000
Preterm birth complications	3,300,000	Colon rectum cancers	2,700,000
Tuberculosis	3,100,000	Diabetes mellitus	2,000,000
Birth asphyxia and birth trauma	2,900,000	Hypertensive heart disease	2,000,000
Protein energy malnutrition	2,700,000	Breast cancer	1,600,000

AIDS and HIV

AIDS (Acquired Immune Deficiency Syndrome) results from damage to the immune system caused by HIV (Human Immunodeficiency Virus) and is now the leading cause of death in the developing world. There are three main ways of contracting the virus: through sexual contact, through infected blood and directly from mother to child.

The World Health Organisation estimates that AIDS has killed about 36 million people since the beginning of the epidemic. In 2012, it killed between 1.4 and 1.9 million people worldwide. It is estimated that 32.2 million to 38.8 million people were currently living with the virus at the end of 2012. There is no known cure, but antiretroviral treatment has substantially increased life expectancy for those who have access to it.

The US Centers for Disease Control and Prevention first reported the illness in Los Angeles in 1981. Current research suggests AIDS originated in sub-Saharan Africa during the twentieth century. Sub-Saharan Africa is the worst affected region in the world, accounting for around 71 per cent of global cases. Lack of resources and education continue to hinder attempts to counter the epidemic.

Prevalence of HIV/AIDS by country

In Swaziland, it is estimated that 26.5 per cent of adults between 15 and 49 have HIV/AIDS, while in Lesotho the number is 23.1 per cent. Botswana is not far behind with 23 per cent. South Africa is at 17.9 per cent, and Zimbabwe is 14.7 per cent. At the other end of the scale, there are scores of countries with death rates below 1 in 100,000. HIV/AIDS is still very rare in some Middle Eastern countries, such as Afghanistan at 0.10 per cent and Saudi Arabia, where its prevalence is estimated at just 0.01 per cent.

Malaria

Malaria is a disease caused by parasites carried by the female anopheles mosquito and transmitted to humans through her bite. There are many different strains of the disease, which is endemic across much of Africa, Asia and South America. Early signs include fever, aching and headache and, if left untreated, the symptoms may worsen and lead to death. Around 90 per cent of malaria fatalities occur in sub-Saharan Africa and the disease accounts for around a fifth of all deaths of African children under five.

In 1907 a Frenchman, Charles Louis Alphonse Laveran, won a Nobel Prize for identifying the causes of malaria. But while there are now drugs that offer us some protection, there is still no known vaccine, and those most at risk often cannot afford the medications that help fight malaria's effects.

Cancer and heart disease

Heart disease is the biggest single killer throughout the world and while our understanding of different variants of cancer grew quickly during the twentieth century, cancer also remains a major cause of death. Rates of many forms of cancer are actually increasing in both developed and developing nations. Death rates from cancer and heart disease are particularly high in southern and eastern Europe, with Hungary suffering the highest prevalence of cancer, and Ukraine the highest prevalence of heart disease.

FACT
The total number of AIDS-related deaths since the syndrome was identified in 1981 has overtaken the worldwide influenza epidemic of 1918–20 and is now second only to the Black Death (bubonic plague) epidemic of the fourteenth century.

Education

Education begins from the moment we are born until the moment we die, taking many forms other than simply that which is taught in a classroom. However, it is widely accepted that formal education is a major factor in a successful society and strong economy. Two basic indicators of the health of a country's education system are its literacy rate and school enrolment figures.

Literacy

Though a blunt measure of educational standards, literacy rates are the most easily available and easily compared yardstick.

"Literate" people are defined as those over the age of 15 who can read and write. Of those countries for which figures are available, more than 120 have literacy rates of over 90 per cent, and eight countries have stated literacy rates of 100 per cent: Andorra, Australia, Denmark, Finland, Liechtenstein, Luxembourg, Norway and Vatican City. Meanwhile, some countries such as Iraq, Senegal, Somalia and Afghanistan have literacy rates of 40 per cent or below. Niger has a literacy rate of less than 20 per cent.

NATIONALITY

What is nationality?

Legal status

Nationality often means a formal, legal relationship between a country and an individual, where the individual agrees to abide by the laws and rules of that country in return for its protection, regardless of where that person is in the world.

The most common way we acquire nationality is through either birthright (*jus soli*) or bloodright (*jus sanguinis*). *Jus soli* gives us a right to citizenship of the country where we were born, while *jus sanguinis* depends on the nationality of a parent. Many countries operate a mixture of both systems, including Canada, Germany, Greece, Ireland, Israel, the United Kingdom and the United States. Citizenship can sometimes be gained via marriage or by naturalisation, which normally involves a period of residency in the new country.

It is possible to belong to more than one country at the same time – to have multiple nationalities – and it is especially common to have dual citizenship. That is to say, you keep your nationality at birth and apply for a

ABOVE Worldwide increases in migration during the twentieth century mean that many young people now have a different nationality to that of their parents.

new one through any of the methods described above. Dual citizenship has many advantages, like being able to work, live or travel in different parts of the world, but it can also have disadvantages. For instance, you may become liable to pay taxes in two different countries or to do military service. While international law does not forbid holding multiple nationalities, only around half of the world's nations allow dual citizenship.

The idea of nationality

For most of us, belonging to a country means much more than simply being part of a legal arrangement. "National identity" might be encapsulated by a particular dish, a song, a sporting moment, a military victory, a political ideal, a person or place or some other symbol altogether. While governments work hard to develop a sense of "national pride," nationalism can unfortunately sometimes turn into xenophobia, where foreigners are regarded with fear or hostility.

The idea of "nation" can be understood to mean any community with aspects of a shared identity, including elements such as shared history, behavioural patterns, language, religion, culture and ethnic origins. This allows certain ethnic groups to see themselves as "nations" despite not having a recognised country or state.

Independence, secession and autonomy

There are many ethnic groups and political movements around the world struggling to win their own country or autonomous region. Some even get as far as operating as *de facto* states, though their sovereignty is disputed or they don"t have international recognition. Below are details of some of the disputes that exist today.

Abkhazia v. Georgia *Abkhazia acts as a* de facto *state but sovereignty is contested by Georgia. Abkhazia has sought membership in the Russian Federation.*

Kosovo v. Serbia *Not technically in dispute, Kosovo declared its independence from Serbia in 2008. It has been recognized by a majority of countries in the European Union and the US. Serbia, however, along with countries like Russia, China and India, does not recognize its independence.*

Nagorno-Karabakh v. Azerbaijan *Nagorno-Karabakh declared itself a de facto state. It is still, however, internationally recognized as a territory of Azerbaijan. Since the end of the Nagorno-Karabakh War in 1994, there have been ongoing peace talks on the disputed situation of the state.*

Palestinian Administered Territories v. Israel *Palestinians want their own state, but negotiations have been unsuccessful largely due to Hamas, its ruling authority and an internationally recognized terrorist organization. Over the years, Israel has agreed to many Palestinian State treaties that were all rejected by Palestinian leaders. In July of 2014, an escalation of actions led to Israel's attempt to remove Hamas from power in the Gaza Strip.*

Somaliland v. Somalia *The Somaliland Republic was declared in 1991. The Somali government failed to reoccupy the territory, but the Republic lacks international recognition. It is a member of the Unrepresented Nations and Peoples Organization.*

South Ossetia v. Georgia *South Ossetia acts as a* de facto *state but sovereignty is contested by Georgia. South Ossetia was officially recognized as an independent state by Russia on August 26, 2008.*

Taiwan v. China *Taiwan has been home to the Nationalist Government of China since Communists seized power on the Chinese mainland in 1949. Taiwan operates as a* de facto *state but China aims for reunification and Taiwan lacks UN recognition.*

Tibet v. China *An autonomous region of China since 1959, Chinese rule of Tibet is contested by the Dalai Lama's "government in exile" in northern India.*

Transnistria v. Moldova *Transnistria lacks international recognition but claimed independence in 1990 with support from Russian troops and acts as a* de facto *state.*

Western Sahara v. Morocco *Officially a semi-autonomous region, sovereignty of Western Sahara is disputed between Morocco and the Polisario Front's "government in exile."*

FACT
In the 1990s, Lyall Sempf declared his own independent nation, the "Principality of Range View," in remote Western Australia. The Australian government has not intervened.

Human Development Index

The Human Development Index (HDI) is a list updated each year by the United Nations to give a snapshot of human development in different countries around the world. While it does not claim to give the complete picture, it works from the premise that humans are a country's most important element and that "human development" is about more than a country's economic wealth. The index measures three main aspects of human development: longevity (measured by life expectancy at birth); knowledge (measured by a combination of adult literacy rate and enrolment in formal education); and standard of living (measured by Gross Domestic Product per capita).

Most of the world is gradually increasing its HDI score, although sub-Saharan Africa and the former Soviet Bloc are actually showing

HDI levels around the world

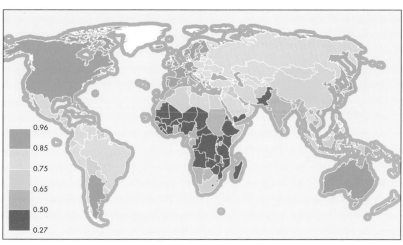

| 0.96 |
| 0.85 |
| 0.75 |
| 0.65 |
| 0.50 |
| 0.27 |

Top and bottom 10 nations by UN HDI ranking in 2013

Country	HDI	Country	HDI
Top ten		Bottom ten	
Norway	0.944	Niger	0.337
Australia	0.933	Democratic Republic of the Congo	0.338
Switzerland	0.917	Central African Republic	0.341
Netherlands	0.915	Chad	0.372
United States	0.914	Sierra Leone	0.374
Germany	0.911	Eritrea	0.381
New Zealand	0.910	Burkina Faso	0.388
Canada	0.902	Burundi	0.389
Singapore	0.901	Guinea	0.392
Denmark	0.900	Mozambique	0.393

a decline. Canada and Norway have topped the list most regularly. Clearly, countries with the highest levels of development are economically wealthy and politically and socially stable, while those near the bottom often have weak economies and unstable or corrupt governments. Many of the countries at the lowest levels have also been plagued by AIDS and war over many years.

A few countries are excluded from the list because the necessary information either does not exist or has not been made available by the relevant governments recently. It is some of these same countries

FACT

The HDI was adopted by the UN in 1993 but was devised in 1990 by Mahbub ul Haq (1934–98), a Pakistani economist who made great contributions to human development in poorer countries. He spent many years working for the World Bank and was also Pakistan's minister for finance and planning. He founded the Human Development Centre, based in Pakistan, in 1996.

FACT
One of the biggest climbers in the latest HDI charts was Saudi Arabia, which leapt from fifty-seventh place in 2012 up to thirty-fourth place in 2013.

that may have particularly low HDIs. These countries include North Korea, South Sudan and Somalia.

The best place to be?

The Economist Intelligence Unit has its own "quality of life" index, taking into account income, health, freedom, unemployment, family life, climate, political stability and security, gender equality and family and community life. Ireland emerged as "the best place in the world to live." Australia was in sixth place but all the other top 10 ranked nations were European: Switzerland, Norway, Luxembourg, Sweden, Iceland, Italy, Denmark and Spain.

You can have an infinite number of reasons for choosing one place over another. For instance, some people might decide to steer clear of Lithuania as it has the highest suicide rate in the world, or Colombia, where you stand the best chance of being kidnapped. The aspiring entrepreneur may instead decide to go to the United States, home to more billionaires than anywhere else, while the environmentally conscious may opt for Switzerland, the country with the best recycling record. Listed below are a few other suggestions of the best places for different people:

For whom?	Where?	Why?
Book worm	India	Most hours per week reading – 10.7
Female politician	Rwanda	Largest percentage of politicians – 49%
Happily married	Colombia	Lowest divorce rate – 0.2%
Plane spotter	Hong Kong	Hong Kong International Airport rated the world's best
Single man	Venezuela	Along with India, home to the most Miss Worlds – 5
Soccer fan	Brazil	Winner of the most World Cups – 5
The thirsty	India	The biggest tea consumers – 561,330 tonnes per year

Religion

A religion is a system of beliefs and worship that helps people give meaning to their lives and understand the world around them. There are a few large, widespread religions that are followed by the majority of the world's population.

Eastern religions

Eastern religions don"t imagine God so much as a personality but rather as a force or power. Believers consider themselves to be on a spiritual journey to enlightenment and rebirth, with meditation and personal experience as key steps on this path. *Taoism* originated in prehistoric China and was formalised into an organised religion around 600 BCE by the philosopher Lao Zi, whose beliefs, sayings and teachings are contained in the *Tao-Te Ching*. *Buddhism* and *Confucianism* were founded in Nepal and China respectively about 100 years later, and all three religions have co-existed since in greater harmony than many other religions. These eastern religions also influenced the Japanese religion of *Shinto*.

Main religions around the world

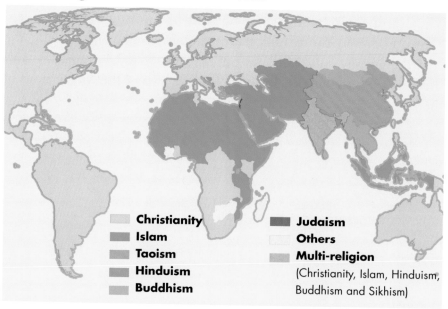

Christianity
Islam
Taoism
Hinduism
Buddhism

Judaism
Others
Multi-religion
(Christianity, Islam, Hinduism, Buddhism and Sikhism)

Monotheistic religions

Monotheistic religions believe in a single, all-powerful God who created the world. Humanity is considered to have "fallen" from the perfection of original creation but can find salvation through faith and by living in accordance with the will of God. According to the Old Testament, Abraham was the father of the Hebrew people, and he is regarded as the founder of the three largest monotheistic faiths (or "Abrahamic" religions). The earliest of these was *Judaism*, the main authority of which is the Hebrew Bible known as the *Tanakh*. The second was *Christianity*, which follows the teachings of Jesus Christ described in the New Testament. The Christian church has split into many different branches over time and now includes many different denominations. *Islam* acknowledges Abraham, Moses and Jesus as prophets but follows the teachings of the *Qur"an* (Koran) as the word of Allah revealed through the prophet Mohammad.

Hinduism, Jainism and Sikhism

India is the birthplace of many religions which, though very different, share certain beliefs. Hinduism has no historical founder but was firmly established as a system of belief by 1200 BCE. It has many gods and goddesses, and followers believe in reincarnation. It preaches high personal moral standards and the idea of *karma* – that we will reap what we sow. *Jainism* evolved from *Hinduism* during the sixth century BCE, following the teachings of the ascetic Vardhamana Jnatriputra, who rejected the authority of the Hindu scriptures but recognised some of Hinduism's deities. *Sikhism* is the youngest of the major religions, and was founded by the guru Nanak around 1500 with the aim of ending conflict, teaching that all religions represent different paths to the same divine Being and should therefore all be respected.

On the next page is a chart of the religious beliefs with the most followers around the world. All the figures are based on what religion people consider themselves to be, though this doesn"t necessarily represent the number of practising followers of each.

Religious adherents globally

Religion	No. of adherents	Religion	No. of adherents
Christianity	2.1 billion	African traditional and diasporic	100 million
Islam	1.3 billion	Sikhism	23 million
Hinduism	900 million	Juche	19 million
Chinese folk religion	394 million	Spiritism	15 million
Buddhism	376 million	Judaism	14 million
Primal indigenous	300 million		

Religions by country

Buddhism *is practised more in China than anywhere else, with 102 million Chinese Buddhists. Next comes Japan, with 90 million adherents, while Thailand, Vietnam and Myanmar also have large Buddhist populations.*

Christianity *has its largest following in the United States, with 224 million believers, followed by 139 million in Brazil. Mexico, Russia and China have the next largest Christian populations.*

Hinduism *has by far its biggest following in India, where there are 751 million Hindus. Nepal and Bangladesh have the only other Hindu populations over 10 million.*

Islam *is most practised in Indonesia, with 170 million followers, though Pakistan, Bangladesh and India are not too far behind.*

Judaism *is most practised in the United States, where there are 6 million believers. The next largest Jewish populations are in Israel and Russia.*

A few countries have practically only one religion. For instance, 98 per cent of the population of Greece are Christian; the populations of both Saudi Arabia and Somalia are virtually 100 per cent Muslim; Nepal is just under 90 per cent Hindu; 94 per cent of Thais claim Buddhist adherence; 80 per cent of Israel's population is Jewish.

Creation myths and sacred texts

Most religions have a "creation myth" or "origin belief" which attempts to explain how the world came into being. Often these creation myths do not sit easily with scientific theory; for instance, many people argue that the Bible's description of creation is irreconcilable with the theory of evolution. Some believers reconcile science and religion by arguing that creation myths should not be read as literal descriptions, but rather as allegorical stories.

All of the major monotheistic religions (Christianity, Islam and Judaism) have broadly similar stories in which a single God figure is responsible for creating the Universe out of nothing. The Book of Genesis describes how "In the Beginning God created the heavens and the Earth" and over the next five days created day and night, sea and lands, birds and beasts and the first humans.

In Hinduism, the existence of the Universe is governed by Brahma, Vishnu and Shiva (the Creator, the Sustainer and the Destroyer) and all living things are considered to be partly divine. Jainism, however, does not believe in a single creation but that the Universe moves through an eternal series of cycles.

Many native peoples have creation myths of their own which are very different from those put forward by organised religion. Among the best known is that of the Australian Aboriginals, who believe in the Dreamtime. This was a time when ancient ancestors walked the world, two of whom, the Ungambikula, discovered half-formed humans made of plants and animals. The Ungambikula fashioned them into complete humans and to this day each man and woman is expected to show allegiance to the animal or plant from which they were created. The Inuits, in turn, believe in creation by a man with a raven's beak, who fixed the lands and seas in place by pecking at water as it burst through the land. Alternatively, the Navajo trace the Earth's evolution through five underworlds, with man and woman said to have been created in the fourth world from ears of corn.

Buddhism attaches little importance to explaining creation, and Buddha himself is said to have commented that trying to understand where we all come from only brings "madness and vexation."

Patron saints

Patron saints come from the Christian tradition and are particularly common in Roman Catholicism and Eastern Orthodoxy. Patron saints are chosen to protect various aspects of human life, including countries, churches, activities, illnesses or good causes. Often some part of the saint's life has some connection to the thing they have been designated to protect. While patron saints are usually chosen by the Pope, other groups and individuals can choose them as well.

Many professional occupations also have their own patrons. Saint Clare of Assisi is the patron saint of television workers. She is said to have been unable to attend Mass one Christmas but had a miraculous vision of the entire service from her sick bed, as if she was seeing it on a television. Saint Ambrose, the patron saint of bee keepers, also has an unusual story. His legend says that a swarm of bees landed on his face when he was a small child, leaving behind a drop of honey. Meanwhile, the patron of dentists is Saint Apollonia, who gruesomely had her teeth pulled out by a mob in the third century.

Selected national patron saints

Country	Saint	Country	Saint
Brazil	Nossa Senhora de Aparecida, Peter of Alcantara	Mexico	Our Lady of Guadalupe
		Norway	Olaf
Canada	Joseph	Poland	Casimir, Cunegund, Stanislas Kostka, Florian
China	Joseph		
England	George	Russia	Andrew, Nicholas of Myra, Therese of Lisieux
France	Our Lady of Assumption, Joan of Arc, Therese of Lisieux		
		Scotland	Andrew, Columba
Germany	Boniface, Michael	Spain	James the Greater, Teresa of Avila
Greece	Andrew, Nicholas	Sweden	Bridget, Eric
Ireland	Patrick, Brigid, Columba	United States	Immaculate Conception of Mary
Italy	Frances of Assisi, Catherine of Siena	Wales	David

FACT
Despite being England's patron, Saint George never went anywhere near the country. His adoption as a symbol of England is probably rooted in the Crusades, when he was held up as an example of chivalric ideals. Edward III founded the Order of the Garter in his name in 1350.

National symbols

Nations have adopted a wide range of symbols and emblems to help their citizens feel a sense of national identity. Some are chosen consciously (like those used in flags, coats of arms or to promote tourism) while others become part of the collective consciousness over a long period of time.

Anthems

Most countries have an official patriotic song that is designated as their national anthem. The Dutch anthem, *Wilhelmus* (written in the late sixteenth century), is generally accepted as the world's oldest anthem. Anthems encompass a range of musical styles but marches and hymns are particularly popular. Anthems tend to be quite short (averaging around a minute and a half) and were often written by relatively little-known composers and lyricists, though there are exceptions. For instance, the German anthem was composed by Joseph Haydn, while the Nobel laureate, Rabindranath Tagore, wrote the words for the anthems of both India and Bangladesh.

FACT
The British anthem, *God Save the King*, and Liechtenstein's *Oben am jungen Rhein* (*Up Above the Young Rhine*), both use the same tune.

Food and drink

Certain dishes and drinks become synonymous with particular nations although the relationship is usually very informal. For instance, apple pie is often associated with the United States, sushi with Japan and so on. Sometimes a national dish is almost imposed upon a nation and becomes a national stereotype, as has happened with France and frog's legs. The French in turn have been known to refer to the English as *les rosbifs* in recognition of the British love of roast beef. Fish and chips is similarly associated with Britain though another popular dish, chicken tikka masala, highlights some of the problems in labelling "national dishes." Widely believed to be a traditional Indian dish, it was in fact especially created by immigrant Indian or Bangladeshi chefs in the late twentieth century to suit the British palate.

Certain drinks also become strongly linked with particular countries. Obvious examples include vodka and Russia, whisky and Scotland and Coca-Cola and the United States. Beer and wine have particularly wide international appeal but in terms of *per capita* consumption, the Czech Republic, Ireland and Germany are the biggest beer drinkers while Luxembourg, France and Italy are the leading wine drinkers.

Natural symbols

Birds, animals, plants and flowers provide many of the most popular emblems of nationhood. For instance, the United States is often represented by the bald eagle, Australia is depicted as a kangaroo, South Africa as a springbok and Russia as a bear. Lions, representing

FACT
The bald eagle, the symbol of the United States, is not actually bald. Rather "bald" is derived from the Old English *balde*, meaning white. The bald eagle was officially classified as endangered in the US between 1967 and 1995. On June 28, 2007 the Service decided to remove the bald eagle from the threatened and endangered list.

bravery and indomitability, are particularly popular and are associated with, among others, Belgium, the Czech Republic, Denmark, Finland, Montenegro, the Netherlands, Singapore, Sweden and Britain. Birds of prey are also common (e.g., Albania, Austria, Egypt and Poland), as are elephants (India, Laos and Thailand).

ABOVE The bald eagle population in the United States has now stabilised.

Among the most recognised national plants are Canada's maple leaf, India's lotus, Ireland's shamrock, the Netherlands" tulip, New Zealand's silver fern, Scotland's thistle and Wales's daffodil. One of the most regularly used is the rose, which has come to be associated with Bulgaria, England, the Maldives and the United States. More rarely, some nations are represented by inanimate objects, such as Ireland and the Celtic harp, Israel and the menorah (a special candelabrum) and Japan and the ray-less Sun.

Languages

Language is any system of human communication and it is estimated that there are between 6,000 and 7,000 major living languages and over 40,000 other language variations and dialects. The scientific study of language is called linguistics.

The major language groups (number of speakers 2005)

Language group	No. of speakers (million)	Language group	No. of speakers (million)
Indo-European	2,562	Austronesian	312
Sino-Tibetan	1,276	Dravidian	222
Niger-Congo	358	Altaic	145
Afro-Asiatic	340	Japanese	123

ABOVE Samples from the some of the world's major writing systems, other than the Latin alphabet, which can be seen everywhere else on this page.

There are just over 250 languages with more than a million worldwide speakers each. Mandarin Chinese is the most widely spoken language, with 1.2 billion people claiming it as their first language. Next comes Spanish with 414 million speakers, English with 335 million, Hindi with 260 million and Arabic with 237 million. The next five most widely spoken are Portuguese, Bengali, Russian, Japanese and Javanese.

Many languages are spoken by or being learned by so few people that they are in danger of dying out. Some linguists predict that up to 3,000 living languages could disappear by the end of this century. Examples of languages under threat include many Native American languages, Australian Aboriginal languages, Curonian (spoken in the Baltic region), Ainu (spoken in Japan), Defaka (spoken in Nigeria) and Sami languages (spoken in Scandinavia and Northern Europe).

Language families

Most human languages belong to a broader language family, a group of languages which derive from a common origin. These "origin" languages are known as protolanguages. If a language cannot be fitted into a broader group, it is called a "language isolate."

Countries of the world

A complete list of the world's nations is provided below with information on population size, Gross Domestic Product per capita (see page 93), the name of the capital city, the main languages and an image of the national flag. Only nation-states recognised by the UN have been included – so disputed or dependent territories are not featured in this table. The nations have been categorised by continent, and ordered from largest population to smallest.

Nation		Population	GDP per capita	Capital	Main languages
Africa					
Nigeria		177,096,000	5,600	Abuja	English, Yoruba, Igbo, Ful, Hausa
Ethiopia		86,614,000	453	Addis Ababa	Amharian, Oromiffa, Gurage
Egypt		84,605,000	3,256	Cairo	Arabic
Democratic Republic of the Congo		74,618,000	261	Kinshasa	French, Lingala
South Africa		52,982,000	7,351	Pretora, Bloemfontein, Cape Town	Afrikaans, English, Ndebele, Swazi, Xhosa, Zulu and other African languages
Tanzania		45,950,000	608	Dodoma	Kiswahili, English
Kenya		43,291,000	942	Nairobi	Swahili, English, Kikuyu, Luo
Algeria		38,295,000	5,347	Algiers	Arabic and Berber
Uganda		35,363,000	551	Kampala	English, Swahili, Luganda

Nation		Population	GDP per capita	Capital	Main languages
Sudan		35,150,000	1,580	Khartoum	Arabic, English
Morocco		32,950,000	2,902	Rabat	Arabic, Berber
Ghana		26,441,000	1,604	Accra	English, Kwa, Gur
Mozambique		24,491,000	565	Maputo	Portuguese, Swahili
Ivory Coast		23,919,000	1,243	Yamoussoukro	French
Madagascar		21,852,000	447	Antananarivo	Malagasy, French
Angola		21,256,000	5,482	Luanda	Portuguese, Bantu languages
Cameroon		20,930,000	1,166	Yaoundé	French, English
Niger		17,493,000	394	Niamey	French, Hausa, Fulfulde
Burkina Faso		17,323,000	651	Ouagadougou	French, Mòoré, Mandinka, Bambara
Mali		16,678,000	699	Bamako	French, Bambara
Malawi		15,316,000	268	Lilongwe	Chichewa, English
Zambia		14,129,000	1,462	Lusaka	English, Bantu languages
Senegal		13,567,000	1,023	Dakar	Wolof, French, Mande languages
Zimbabwe		13,098,000	714	Harare	English, Bantu languages
Chad		12,948,000	1,035	N'Djamena	French, Arabic

Nation		Population	GDP per capita	Capital	Main languages
Guinea		11,861,000	491	Conakry	French, Fula, Maninka, Susu
Tunisia		10,889,000	4,236	Tunis	Arabic, French, Berber
Rwanda		10,780,000	619	Kigali	Kinyarwanda, French, English
South Sudan		10,334,000	943	Juba	English, Bari, Dinka, Murle, Nuer, Zande
Benin		9,742,000	752	Porto-Novo	French, Fon, Yoruba
Somalia		9,662,000	145	Mogadishu	Somali, Arabic
Burundi		9,023,000	251	Bujumbura	Kirundi, French, Swahili
Togo		6,675,000	574	Lomé	French, Ewe, Kotocoli, Kabiyé
Libya		6,323,000	10,455	Tripoli	Arabic, Berber
Sierra Leone		5,823,000	634	Freetown	English, Temne, Mende, Krio
Central African Republic		5,217,000	482	Bangui	Sangho, French
Eritrea		4,980,000	504	Asmara	Tigrinya, Arabic, English
Congo, Republic of the		4,525,000	3,154	Brazzaville	French, Kongo, Lingala
Liberia		3,881,000	414	Monrovia	English, Liberian Kreyol
Mauritania		3,461,000	1,106	Nouakchott	Arabic, French, Pulaar, Soninke, Wolof

Nation	Population	GDP per capita	Capital	Main languages
Gabon	2,204,000	11,256	Libreville	French, Fang, Bantu languages
Namibia	2,170,000	5,786	Windhoek	English, German, Bantu languages, Afrikaans
Botswana	2,096,000	7,238	Gaborone	Setswana, English
Lesotho	1,887,000	1,193	Maseru	Sesotho, English
Equatorial Guinea	1,837,000	24,035	Malabo	Spanish, French, Portuguese
The Gambia	1,794,000	506	Banjul	English, Mandinka
Guinea-Bissau	1,699,000	494	Bissau	Portuguese, Crioulo
Mauritius	1,273,000	8,120	Port Louis	Creole, English, French
Swaziland	1,077,000	3,042	Mbabane	Siswati, English
Djibouti	912,000	1,062	Djibouti City	Arabic, French, Somali
Comoros	743,000	831	Moroni	Comorian, Arabic, French
Cape Verde	511,000	3,695	Praia	Portuguese, Crioulo
São Tomé and Principe	194,000	1,400	São Tomé	Portuguese, Forro, Angolar, Principense
Seychelles	94,000	12,783	Victoria	Creole, English, French
Asia				
China	1,357,379,000	6,091	Beijing	Chinese (including variations)

Nation		Population	GDP per capita	Capital	Main languages
India		1,257,476,000	1,503	New Delhi	Hindi, English
Indonesia		248,731,000	3,557	Jakarta	Bahasa Indonesia, Javanese
Pakistan		183,936,000	1,257	Islamabad	Punjan, Urdu, English, Pushtu, Sindh
Bangladesh		154,514,000	752	Dhaka	Bengali, English
Japan		127,350,000	46,731	Tokyo	Japanese
Philippines		98,000,005	2,587	Manila	Filipino, Tagalog, Cebuano
Vietnam		89,702,000	1,755	Hanoi	Vietnamese
Iran		77,789,000	7,228	Tehran	Persian, Turkmen, Kurdish
Thailand		67,357,000	5,480	Bangkok	Thai
Turkey		76,668,000	10,666	Ankara	Turkish, Kurdish
Myanmar		62,342,000	1,200	Naypyidaw	Burmese
South Korea		50,394,000	22,589	Seoul	Korean
Iraq		35,404,000	6,625	Baghdad	Arabic, Kurdish
Malaysia		30,476,000	10,432	Kuala Lumpur	Malay, Chinese
Uzbekistan		30,214,000	1,717	Tashkent	Uzbek, Russian
Saudi Arabia		30,193,000	25,136	Riyadh	Arabic
Nepal		27,224,000	690	Kathmandu	Nepali, Tharu, Tamang

Nation		Population	GDP per capita	Capital	Main languages
Afghanistan		25,758,000	687	Kabul	Pashto, Dari
North Korea		25,313,000	1,800	Pyongyang	Korean
Yemen		25,252,000	1,494	Sana'a	Arabic
Syria		22,169,000	2,065	Damascus	Arabic
Sri Lanka		20,462,000	2,923	Colombo	Sinhala, Tamil
Kazakhstan		17,030,000	12,120	Astana	Kazakh, Russian
Cambodia		14,572,000	944	Phnom Penh	Khmer
Azerbaijan		9,494,600	7,165	Baku	Azerbaijani, Russian
United Arab Emirates		8,659,000	41,691	Abu Dhabi	Arabic
Israel		8,047,000	32,567	Jerusalem	Hebrew, Arabic
Tajikistan		8,044,000	953	Dushanbe	Tajik, Russian
Laos		6,581,000	1,417	Vientiane	Lao
Jordan		6,517,000	4,909	Amman	Arabic
Kyrgyzstan		5,717,000	1,154	Bishkek	Kyrgyz, Russian
Turkmenistan		5,463,000	6,798	Ashgabat	Turkmenian
Singapore		5,437,000	51,709	Singapore	Mandarin, Malay, English
Lebanon		4,127,000	9,705	Beirut	Arabic
Oman		3,942,000	23,569	Muscat	Arabic
Kuwait		3,852,000	56,374	Kuwait City	Arabic

Nation		Population	GDP per capita	Capital	Main languages
Mongolia		2,859,000	3,673	Ulaan Baatar	Mongolian
Qatar		1,917,000	93,825	Doha	Arabic
Bahrain		1,546,000	23,040	Manama	Arabic
Timor-Leste		1,210,000	1,068	Dili	Portuguese, Tetum
Bhutan		728,000	2,399	Thimphu	Dzongkha
Brunei		407,000	41,127	Bandar Seri Begawan	Malay, English
Maldives		331,000	6,567	Malé	Dhivehi
Europe					
Russia		146,068,400	14,037	Moscow	Russian
Germany		80,586,000	42,625	Berlin	German
France		66,475,000	39,771	Paris	French
United Kingdom		64,097,000	38,920	London	English
Italy		59,862,000	33,837	Rome	Italian
Spain		46,610,000	28,292	Madrid	Spanish, Catalan, Basque
Ukraine		45,461,000	3,867	Kiev	Ukrainian, Russian
Poland		38,548,000	12,710	Warsaw	Polish
Romania		19,858,000	8,437	Bucharest	Romanian
Netherlands		16,795,000	29,371	Amsterdam	Dutch
Belgium		11,162,000	43,427	Brussels	Dutch, French, German

Nation		Population	GDP per capita	Capital	Main languages
Greece		10,758,000	22,456	Athens	Greek
Portugal		10,609,000	25,448	Lisbon	Portuguese
Czech Republic		10,519,000	18,690	Prague	Czech
Hungary		9,894,000	12,560	Budapest	Hungarian
Sweden		9,595,000	55,039	Stockholm	Swedish
Belarus		9,460,000	6,685	Minsk	Belarusian, Russian
Austria		8,477,000	46,822	Vienna	German
Switzerland		8,075,000	78,927	Bern	German, French, Italian, Romansh
Bulgaria		7,261,000	6,977	Sofia	Bulgarian
Serbia		7,203,000	5,189	Belgrade	Serbian
Denmark		5,612,000	56,364	Copenhagen	Danish
Finland		5,436,000	45,723	Helsinki	Finnish, Swedish
Slovakia		5,413,000	16,856	Bratislava	Slovak
Norway		5,077,000	99,636	Oslo	Norwegian
Georgia		4,942,000	3,507	Tbilisi	Georgian
Ireland		4,662,000	45,951	Dublin	Irish, English
Croatia		4,258,000	13,878	Zagreb	Croatian
Bosnia and Herzegovina		3,847,000	4,556	Sarajevo	Bosnian, Croatian, Serbian

Nation	Population	GDP per capita	Capital	Main languages
Moldova	3,486,000	2,037	Chișinău	Romanian, Ukrainian, Russian
Armenia	3,018,000	3,351	Yerevan	Armenian
Lithuania	2,956,000	14,172	Vilnius	Lithuanian
Albania	2,783,000	3,999	Tirana	Albanian
Macedonia	2,066,000	4,565	Skopje	Macedonian, Albanian
Slovenia	2,062,000	22,011	Ljubljana	Slovene
Latvia	2,011,000	13,947	Riga	Latvian, Russian
Estonia	1,283,000	16,843	Tallinn	Estonian, Russian
Cyprus	1,117,000	26,070	Lefkosia (Nicosia)	Greek, Turkish
Montenegro	620,000	7,041	Podgorica	Montenegrin, Serbian, Bosnian
Luxembourg	542,000	103,925	Luxembourg City	Lëtzebuergesch, French, German
Malta	419,000	20,793	Valletta	Maltese, English
Iceland	324,000	42,339	Reykjavik	Icelandic
Andorra	75,000	46,418	Andorra la Vella	Catalan, Spanish, French, Portuguese
Liechtenstein	37,000	134,617	Vaduz	German
Monaco	36,000	163,025	Monaco	French
San Marino	32,000	62,188	San Marino	Italian

Nation		Population	GDP per capita	Capital	Main languages
Vatican City		800	25,500	Vatican City	Italian
North America					
United States		316,102,000	51,748	Washington, DC	English, Spanish
Mexico		118,419,000	9,749	Mexico City	Spanish
Canada		35,236,000	51,206	Ottawa, Ontario	English, French
Guatemala		15,440,000	3,330	Guatemala City	Spanish
Cuba		11,163,000	6,051	Havana	Spanish
Haiti		10,671,000	770	Port-au-Prince	French, Creole
Dominican Republic		9,745,000	5,746	Santo Domingo	Spanish
Honduras		8,578,000	2,323	Tegucigalpa	Spanish
El Salvador		6,635,000	3,789	San Salvador	Spanish
Nicaragua		6,216,000	1,753	Managua	Spanish
Costa Rica		4,667,000	9,386	San José	Spanish
Panama		3,605,000	9,534	Panama City	Spanish
Jamaica		2,715,000	5,449	Kingston	English
Trinidad and Tobago		1,344,000	17,437	Port-of-Spain	English
Bahamas, The		368,000	21,908	Nassau	English
Belize		340,000	4,721	Belmopan	English
Barbados		276,000	14,917	Bridgetown	English

Nation		Population	GDP per capita	Capital	Main languages
Saint Lucia		170,000	6,848	Castries	English, Patois
Grenada		103,000	7,267	St. George's	English
Saint Vincent and the Grenadines		97,000	6,515	Kingstown	English
Antigua and Barbuda		88,000	12,733	Saint John's	English
Dominica		71,000	5,745	Roseau	English
Saint Kitts and Nevis		55,000	14,314	Basseterre	English, Creole
South America					
Brazil		201,033,000	11,340	Brasília	Portuguese
Colombia		47,130,000	7,748	Bogotá	Spanish
Argentina		41,350,000	11,573	Buenos Aires	Spanish
Peru		30,476,000	6,796	Lima	Spanish, Quechua
Venezuela		29,760,000	12,729	Caracas	Spanish
Chile		16,841,000	15,452	Santiago	Spanish
Ecuador		15,779,000	5,425	Quito	Spanish
Bolivia		10,517,000	2,576	Sucre	Spanish, Quechua, Aymara
Paraguay		6,849,000	3,813	Asunción	Spanish
Uruguay		3,297,000	4,703	Montevideo	Spanish
Guyana		798,000	3,584	Georgetown	English, Creole

Nation		Population	GDP per capita	Capital	Main languages
Suriname		539,000	9,376	Paramaribo	Dutch, Sranan Tongo Creole
Oceania					
Australia		23,105,000	67,442	Canberra	English
Papua New Guinea		7,461,000	2,184	Port Moresby	Hiri Motu, Tok Pisin, English
New Zealand		4,543,000	38,637	Wellington	English, Maori
Fiji		862,000	4,467	Suva	Fijian, Hindi, English
Solomon Islands		561,000	1,835	Honiara	English
Vanuatu		265,000	3,183	Port Vila	Bislama, English, French
Samoa		190,000	3,620	Apia	Samoan, English
Kiribati		106,000	1,736	South Taraw	English, Gilbertese
Tonga		104,000	4,494	Nuku"alofa	Tongan, English
Micronesia		101,000	3,154	Palikir	English
Marshall Islands		56,000	3,471	Majuro	Marshallese, English
Palau		21,000	11,006	Ngerulmud	English, Palauan
Tuvalu		11,000	4,044	Funafuti	Tuvaluan, English
Nauru		10,000	5,000	Yaren	Nauruan, English

GOVERNMENT

Heads of state

A head of state is the main public representative of a nation. This is usually an individual person but sometimes it can be a collective office, like the one in Bosnia-Herzegovina. The amount of power a head of state has varies from country to country, but they are almost always expected to be a symbol of the country's values and to work to promote the country on the international stage. The most common titles for heads of state are king, queen, president and governor-general.

Even if not the centre of executive power, a head of state will be expected to fulfil many roles. As well as being a national symbol of unity and an important player in diplomatic relations, they are often expected to sign legislation into law, make key state appointments, summon and dissolve legislative bodies and be the nominal head of the national military.

Presidential (or imperial) system: *Like that of the United States, has one person as both head of state and head of government.*

Semi-presidential system: *Of the type used in Russia and Egypt, where the head of state shares executive power with a separate head of government.*

Theoretical executive power: *The United Kingdom has a head of state who possesses theoretical executive power, while in reality, power lies with the head of government.*

Non-executive head of state: *Like that in Ireland, where the head of state is a public face for the nation but has little real power.*

FACT

The longest documented reign of any king is that of King Louis XIV who spent 72 years on the French throne between 1643 and 1715. King Mihti of Arakan (Myanmar) is supposed to have reigned between 1279 and 1374.

If the crown fits...

The world's current longest-serving head of state is Thailand's King Bhumibol Adulyadej, who was crowned on 5 May 1950.

The longest-serving president in the world today is El Hadj Omar Bongo of Gabon, who became president in December 1967. Until his death in February 2005, Togo's General Gnassingbé Eyadéma was the longest-serving, having seized control in a military coup in April 1967.

Fidel Castro only officially became Cuba's president in 1976, but has been that country's effective centre of power since 1959.

Heads of government

A head of government is the leader of a national government or cabinet. This may sometimes be the same person as the head of state, especially in a presidential system or an absolute monarchy. The most common methods by which the head of government leaves office are by resigning, dying, losing a party leadership vote, losing a parliamentary vote of confidence or losing a budget vote. Very occasionally, a head of state will dismiss a democratically elected head of government.

In semi-presidential systems, the head of state might have responsibility for choosing the head of government but will probably choose the leader of the most popular political party at that moment, regardless of their personal preference.

In a parliamentary system, the head of government is usually called prime minister, first minister or premier, and is the focus of executive power.

In parliamentary democracies, the head of government will normally be the leader of the most-voted-for political party and will be responsible for the conduct of government. A few countries leave parliament to elect the head of government itself.

FACT
Sirimavo Bandaranaike became the world's first female head of government when she was elected Prime Minister of Sri Lanka in 1960. She went on to serve three separate terms and her daughter, Chandrika Kumaratunga, became Sri Lanka's first female president in 1994. The world's first woman president was Isabel Perón, who took office in Argentina in 1974.

Power sharing

Many countries operate a system of government where power is split between an executive, a legislature and a judiciary. Each arm has particular powers and areas of responsibility to ensure that no one part of government becomes too powerful.

Executive branch: *(the head of government, cabinet and government ministries) looks after the day-to-day business of government.*

Legislature: *(parliament, congress or national assembly) adopts laws, decides on a budget for government finance and expenditure and usually has to give its consent to major actions like declaring war.*

Judiciary: *(the system of courts) is there to interpret the law.*

Puppet governments

While every country theoretically has a right to its own independent government, this is not always the case. A government that is, to all intents and purposes, under the control of a foreign government is called a "puppet regime."

One of the most infamous was the Norwegian government of Vidkun Quisling, which collaborated with Adolf Hitler's Germany from 1943–45. Quisling is used in the English language to mean someone who collaborates with a hostile occupying force.

Systems of government

Many different systems of government are used throughout the world, some of which differ only in details and others which are fundamentally opposed. Most countries do not have "pure" systems of government but combine aspects from several different models.

Autocracy

Autocracy is absolute and unlimited rule by an individual, and is manifested in countries governed by despotism or dictatorship. An autocrat is likely to govern through force or fear as a means of removing opposition, although it is possible for an autocrat to rise to power by democratic methods. History is filled with autocrats, dictators and despots, and the reigns of two such figures, Hitler and Stalin, left deep scars on the twentieth century.

Democracy

Democracy is a system of government by the common people. In its purest form, democracy means supreme power is exercised by the people themselves; but in practice, power is given to "democratic representatives" chosen in elections.

In a democracy, government is regarded as a political body that should serve the people rather than rule over them. The world's largest functioning democracy is India.

Federalism

Federalism describes government where power is shared between a central power and constituent political units, such as states or provinces. Only 25 countries have federal systems but their citizens make up 40 per cent of the world's population. They include Argentina, Australia, Brazil, Canada, Germany, India, Malaysia, Mexico, Nigeria, Pakistan, Russia, South Africa, Spain and the United States.

Federal states often experience friction between the central government and the local political units. The European Union is at the centre of an important on-going argument as to whether or not it is federalist at all.

Monarchy

Monarchy is rule by a king, queen, emperor or empress. Royal power is often inherited. An absolute monarchy is one where the monarch is all-powerful, like the seventeenth- and eighteenth-century French King, Louis XIV. Absolute monarchies still exist in several countries, including Brunei, Saudi Arabia and Swaziland. Other countries, such as Qatar, Bhutan, Liechtenstein, Jordan, Tonga and Kuwait are no longer absolute monarchies but still have very powerful royal

ABOVE Louis XIV of France.

heads of state. Many monarchies have had their power limited over time, such as that in Britain, and are called constitutional monarchies.

Plutocracy

Plutocracy is government by the wealthiest sector of society. Anti-democratic by its nature, no nation claims to be a plutocracy but some analysts argue that the influence of "big business" over governments throughout the world is a form of plutocracy.

FACT

The world's oldest existing national legislative body is Iceland's parliament, the Althingi, established in 930 CE. The meeting of the Althingi constitutes the historical basis of the Icelandic nation, and in its early form it was open to all the free men of the land.

Military government

Military government often results from *coups d"etat*, where a national army removes the existing government and takes over power itself. Often, though not always, military government develops into military dictatorship, under leaders such as Idi Amin in Uganda and Augusto Pinochet in Chile. Historically, Latin America, Africa and the Middle East have been particularly susceptible to military dictatorships.

Pluralism

Pluralism is government by a range of competing groups (such as Church, business and the labour force), who arrive at political decisions by bargaining and compromising. No one organisation controls the balance of power, and the process of discussion is meant to protect the rights and interests of everyone. In many ways, it is an extension of the democratic ideal and most countries would claim to be, at least in part, pluralist.

Republicanism

Republicanism is where political power is in the hands of a government chosen by popular election. Government power is limited by law, often in the form of a constitution. Many countries without a monarchy have come to be known as republics, even though they might actually operate a different system altogether.

Theocracy

Theocracy is government by religious officials and where religion plays the dominant role in political life. Perhaps the most famous modern example is that of Iran, which became a theocracy when Ayatollah Khomeini came to power in 1979. The Taliban regime in Afghanistan was also a theocracy. Though theocracies have little history in the West, it is often argued that Vatican City has theocratic characteristics.

Political philosophies

Political philosophies look at the fundamental questions of law and government. Political arguments and public debate are largely based on conflicting allegiances to these philosophical ideals.

Conservatism: *The umbrella term for a range of philosophies that broadly promote traditional values and the established social order. In recent times, conservatism has become linked with right-of-centre politics, but this is not always the case. While conservatism does not rule out any change to the status quo, it prefers change to happen gradually.*

Liberalism: *Prizes individual liberty as the highest political value. Classical liberalism, which had its golden age in nineteenth-century Europe, demanded freedom from too much interference from Church and State authority. It also promoted free thought, free enterprise economics and parliamentary democracy. Modern liberalism, however, tends to support some government intervention in the economy to ensure a basic level of welfare for everyone. The influence of liberalism waned in the twentieth century in the face of the ideological battles between socialism, communism, fascism and conservatism.*

Fascism: *As epitomised by Benito Mussolini's Italy in the first half of the twentieth century, it demands that the individual is secondary to the nation. Characteristics of fascism include extreme national pride, a focus on military might and authoritarian government at the expense of parliamentary democracy. With its totalitarian attempts to impose control and its links with Hitler's Nazis, fascism is rarely openly championed in contemporary politics.*

Capitalism: *Strives for a society where everything is privately owned and run, with the aim of creating profit for private individuals. While most of the developed world is broadly capitalist, very few countries have absolutely no state ownership and no economic intervention by the government.*

FACT
Kibbutzim are collective communities unique to Israel, based on common ownership of the means of production and consumption. Since 1909, when the first kibbutz was established at Deganya, kibbutz communities have successfully combined socialism and Zionism to play a major role in the social and economic life of the Jewish state.

Socialism: *Promotes state ownership of the means of production and exchange (that is to say, the tools for industry and trade) so they can be used in the interests of all the people. Socialism in its purest form is directly opposed to capitalism but many socialists now embrace elements of both.*

Communism *is a branch of socialism which believes in a classless society based upon common ownership of the means of production. Some communist ideologies see a "class war" between the proletariat (the workers) and the capital-owning classes as inevitable. Communism as a practical system of government was largely discredited by the experiences of the twentieth century and even China, the world's largest communist state, has started to open up its economy.*

Anarchism: *Argues that all government should be abolished and that laws, authority and rulers are unnecessary. Instead, society would function by self-government and voluntary co-operation between individuals.*

Environmentalism: *Concerns itself with the rights and needs of the planet and non-human species, as opposed to the traditional focus on human development. Environmentalism not only emphasises the rights of non-human species but also the benefits to mankind in working towards the greater good of the planet.*

Suffrage

Suffrage is the right to vote in political elections. Universal suffrage, where all adults are entitled to vote regardless of race, gender, wealth, creed or social status, is a widely held ideal. Some countries, notably Australia, operate a system of compulsory suffrage, where everyone who is qualified to vote is obliged to do so.

It is only quite recently that many social groups have won the right to vote. It used to be the case in many countries that voters had to prove they had a certain level of wealth or literacy before they could enter the ballot box, ensuring that suffrage remained with only a select section of society. It is still common for the vote to be denied on grounds of mental capacity or criminal convictions. The minimum age for voting in most parts of the world is between 15 and 21.

Women's suffrage in particular took a long time to establish. In 1893, New Zealand became the first country to grant women the vote. It was not until 1918 that British and German women were enfranchised while American females had to wait till 1920 and Kuwaitis until 1984!

International organisations

There are many organisations working throughout the world to overcome international political, economic, social, cultural and humanitarian troubles. Outlined below are just a few of the biggest and most influential.

The United Nations

The UN is an association of nations that have pledged to maintain international peace and to work together to solve international problems. American President Franklin D. Roosevelt came up with the name "United Nations" and it was used for the first time in 1942 when 26 nations promised to continue the fight against the Axis Powers in the Second World War. The UN was a natural successor to the League of Nations established after the First World War.

The United Nations Charter was drawn up by representatives of 50 countries in 1945, based on a framework constructed by China, the Soviet Union, the United Kingdom and the United States during 1944. There are now 191 member states – only Vatican City is not a member. United Nations Day is celebrated on 24 October each year.

Around 80 per cent of the UN's work is devoted to helping developing countries build the capacity to help themselves, through promoting independent and democratic societies, protecting human rights, assisting refugees and victims of starvation, war and natural disaster, and countering global crime, drugs and disease. The Charter does not allow for intervention in any state's essentially domestic issues.

North Atlantic Treaty Organisation
NATO is the executive arm of the North Atlantic Alliance, an alliance of countries established in 1949 in accordance with the terms of the UN Charter. It works towards maintaining international security through political and, if necessary, military means. At the moment NATO has troops trying to keep the peace in Afghanistan, Kosovo and the Mediterranean Sea.

■ NATO members
□ Original NATO members

ABOVE The original NATO members were Belgium, Canada, Denmark, France, Iceland, Italy, Luxembourg, the Netherlands, Norway, Portugal, Britain and the United States. Later additions have brought the total membership up to 28 nations.

The European Union

The EU is a community of European nations that has evolved since the 1950s from the initial hope of bringing Europe's nations together after the Second World War. Winston Churchill called for a "united states of Europe" in 1946 and chaired the 1948 congress that created the Council of Europe. The community developed with the establishment of the European Coal and Steel Community in 1951, and the European Economic Community, and Atomic Energy Community in 1957. In 1992, the Maastricht Treaty defined the goal of the EU as "an ever closer union among the peoples of Europe, in which decisions are taken as closely as possible to the citizen." In reality, though, the work of the EU has been hindered by arguments between member states who want different levels of cooperation. There are currently 28 members of the EU.

EU membership timeline

Year	Country
1952	Belgium, France, West Germany, Italy, Luxembourg, the Netherlands (founding members)
1973	Denmark, Ireland, United Kingdom
1981	Greece
1986	Portugal, Spain
1990	East Germany reunites with West Germany and becomes part of the EU
1995	Austria, Finland, Sweden
2004	Cyprus, Czech Republic, Estonia, Hungary, Latvia, Lithuania, Malta, Poland, Slovakia, Slovenia
2007	Bulgaria, Romania
2013	Croatia

Albania, Iceland, Montenegro, Serbia, Macedonia and Turkey are all in talks with the EU about becoming members.

The EU includes around 500 million people and covers an area of over 4.3 million sq km (1.6 million square miles). Around 1.5 per cent of the EU's population now live in a different country from their country of origin. When membership grew to

ABOVE Inside the European Parliament in Brussels, Belgium.

include 10 countries from Central and Eastern Europe in 2004, some people feared an unmanageable influx of immigrants from these countries to wealthier western neighbours, but figures suggest this has not happened – workers from new member countries account for less than 1 per cent of the working age population in the older member states, apart from Austria (1.4 per cent) and Ireland (3.8 per cent).

English is the single most widely spoken language in Europe – around 34 per cent of EU inhabitants can speak it. Over 50 per cent of the EU population can speak at least one foreign language and in several countries – the Baltic states, Denmark, Luxembourg, Malta, the Netherlands and Sweden – this figure rises to 87 per cent. Perhaps because they can rely on other countries speaking English, the United Kingdom seems rather lazy in learning other tongues – only around 30 per cent speak a foreign language.

The EU outlaws any economic discrimination by nationality and rules that men and women should receive equal pay. One of the biggest projects of the EU is to develop a single internal market and bring the economies of member countries up to a similar level. It also plays a role in agricultural, environmental and transportation issues.

Military defence

National armed forces

Most nations take responsibility for their own national defence, usually through three main military branches: an army, an air force and a navy. North Korea focuses more on defence than any other country, with 25 per cent of the nation's GDP spent on its military.

International peacekeeping

The United Nations plays an important role in securing and maintaining peace in conflict areas around the world. As of June 2014, the UN had overseen 69 peacekeeping operations since 1948, in which almost 3,250 UN personnel had lost their lives.

Notable U.N. peacekeeping missions

Types of mission	Year started	Number of personnel (approx.)
Truce Supervision Organisation (Middle East)	1948	370
Military Observer Group in India and Pakistan	1949	115
Peacekeeping Force in Cyprus	1964	1,050
Disengagement Observer Force (Golan Heights)	1974	1,200
Interim Force in Lebanon	1978	2,400
Mission for the Referendum in Western Sahara	1991	450
Observer Mission in Georgia	1993	430
Interim Administration Mission in Kosovo	1999	5,700
Organisation Mission in the Congo, Dem. Rep.	1999	19,600
Mission in Ethiopia and Eritrea	2000	3,850
Mission in Liberia	2003	17,700
Operation in Côte d'Ivoire	2004	8,600
Stabilisation Mission in Haiti	2004	10,400
Operation in Burundi	2004	6,250
Mission in Sudan	2005	8,000

FACT
China has the largest armed forces in the world, numbering around 2,285,000 personnel. The next biggest is the United States (1,369,532), then India (1,325,000), North Korea (1,210,000) and Russia (766,000).

Nuclear weapons

With the end of the Cold War, many analysts thought that the threat of nuclear war would diminish but sadly, we still live under its shadow. The Nuclear Non-Proliferation Treaty (NNPT), drafted in 1968, sets limits on the possession of nuclear weapons and has been signed by 188 countries. It recognises five confirmed nuclear states: China, France, Russia, the United Kingdom and the United States. India and Pakistan have also carried out test explosions and Israel is thought to have usable nuclear weapons, while Iran is suspected by much of the international community of trying to get them. North Korea has claimed to have an arsenal though the truth of that is not completely clear. India, Israel and Pakistan are among the small group of nations not to have signed the NNPT.

Below is a table of known and suspected nuclear arsenals around the world. Not surprisingly, most countries keep the exact details of their nuclear weapons quiet, so these figures are estimates.

Nuclear arsenals

Country	Estimated no. of warheads	Country	Estimated no. of warheads
China	250	Pakistan	110
France	300	Russia	8,000
India	110	United Kingdom	225
Israel	80	United States	7,315
North Korea	9		

Espionage

Espionage, the art of spying on rival states, is practised throughout the world but rarely discussed by governments. The aim of espionage is to gain economic, political or military advantage and attempts to defend against it are called counter-espionage. Fictional spies like James Bond have ensured that we have come to see spying as a dangerous but glamorous game. Among the world's most famous intelligence agencies are the United States" CIA, Britain's MI5 and MI6, the Soviet Union's KGB (superseded by the SVR in Russia) and the Mossad of Israel. But it is not only countries that involve themselves in spying. Industrial espionage between businesses has become a serious problem for many companies.

Spying has gone on through the ages and there is evidence of it in both ancient China and ancient Egypt. By the Middle Ages, there were intelligence organisations working throughout Europe. In the twentieth century, the two World Wars gave rise to many famous acts of espionage but for many, the Cold War was the "golden age" of spying.

Following the collapse of communism, the United States now focuses its intelligence gathering on international drugs suppliers, and the terrorist networks that were involved in the 9/11 attacks on New York and Washington, DC.

FACT

The Enigma cipher was key to German military and intelligence communications during the Second World War until it was broken in 1940 by British and Polish mathematicians. The odds of anyone breaking the code when not in possession of the correct Enigma machine settings was put at 150 million million million to one.

Law enforcement

Frontline maintenance of law and order falls to the police in most nations. There is some debate as to which is the oldest organised, professional, non-military police force. The Metropolitan Police, serving London, was established in 1829 but the British Transport Police can trace its roots back to 1826, while the City of Glasgow Police in Scotland was founded in 1800.

Largest police force, crime rate and prison populations

Police personnel per 100,000 pop.		Recorded crimes per 100,000 pop.		Prisoners per 100,000 pop.	
Kuwait	1,116	Iceland	21,211	United States	714
Cyprus	618	Sweden	13,837	Belarus	532
Italy	559	United Kingdom	11,014	Russia	532
Uruguay	541	Finland	10,005	Turkmenistan	489
Panama	519	Belgium	9,442	Cuba	487

Road rules

A major aspect of modern policing is controlling how people behave on the roads. Speed is a particular problem, as improvements in engineering have created cars that are capable of travelling much faster than is safe or reasonable. Indeed, road accidents are a major cause of death, especially in developed countries (see p. 41). While some small countries combat this by posting blanket speed limits as low as 60 km/h (37 mph – in Monaco and Barbados), there are *autobahnen* in Germany where there is no speed limit, and it is not uncommon for cars to travel at over 200 km/h (125 mph).

In the majority of countries, everyone must drive on the right-hand side, but there are 53 countries that drive on the left. Britain is a "left-hand side" country and spread that system via its empire. Therefore, countries that drive on the left are mostly previous members of the British Empire, while countries colonised by France, Spain or Portugal drive on the right.

Strange laws

Governments make laws to help and protect us. Or at least that is usually the case, but there are plenty of laws around the world that just seem to make life more complicated. Sometimes these are ancient laws which have never been repealed and which reflect the standards of a different age. Sometimes they are just plain odd.

In Britain: *It remains illegal to wear armour in Parliament, to bet or gamble in a library reading room or to use "any slide upon ice or snow." For a long time it was also a requirement for able-bodied males between the ages of 16 and 60 to practise their archery after church on Sundays.*

In the United States: *Ohio outlaws getting a fish drunk, while in Fairbanks, Alaska, it is apparently illegal to feed a moose any alcoholic beverage. Meanwhile, in New York, you need a licence for an outdoor clothesline.*

In Canada: *Businesses in Calgary are required to have a hitching post for tying up horses outside their premises.*

In Denmark: *On the road, drivers are required to make a visual check for any stray children under the car before starting the engine. Less understandably, there should be someone in front of the car to wave a flag as a warning to oncoming horse-drawn carriages.*

In Australia: *Taxi cabs must carry a bale of hay in the boot.*

In Hong Kong: *A wronged wife in Hong Kong is theoretically allowed to kill her adulterous husband as long as she does it with her bare hands!*

FACT
Animal trials became relatively common during the Middle Ages, often on charges related to witchcraft. As recently as 1906, Switzerland was the setting for a murder carried out by two men "with the fierce and effective co-operation of their dog."

ECONOMY

Developed and developing nations

The "developed world" is a term used for those countries with mature, highly industrialised economies. According to some analysts, the developed world is a very select group comprised of the nations of Western Europe, the United States, Canada, Japan, Israel, Australia and New Zealand. But there is no globally accepted set of qualification criteria and other analysts insist that extra factors should be taken into account, such as human and civil rights, health, education and welfare.

Between the 1950s and the 1990s, the terms First World, Second World and Third World were more commonly used. The "First World" originally referred to North America, Western Europe and other leading capitalist countries, such as Australia, Canada, Japan, New Zealand and South Africa. The "Second World" included the Soviet Union and the rest of the Eastern Bloc communist countries

ABOVE The system of dividing the world into First, Second and Third worlds derived from the Cold War (1940s to 1980s), during which much of the world was ideologically and militarily divided into capitalist West and communist East.

while the "Third World" was comprised of all those countries not covered by the first two classifications. These were very approximate groupings and many countries did not fit comfortably under any of the labels. The end of the Soviet Union made the term "Second World" redundant and "First World" came to be used for developed nations while the "Third World" referred to the less developed.

Gross Domestic Product

Gross Domestic Product (GDP) is the most widely used measure of a country's economic performance. It is calculated as the total value of all goods and services produced within a nation's borders during a given year. It is sometimes used as an indicator of standard of living – when GDP increases, it is taken to mean that the standard of living will have done so too. But this is based on a narrow view of living standards and other indicators give a broader picture of quality of life (see Human Development Index, p. 49). However, GDP is calculated consistently and regularly throughout the world, making it the best single indicator of a country's economic health.

GDP per capita around the world

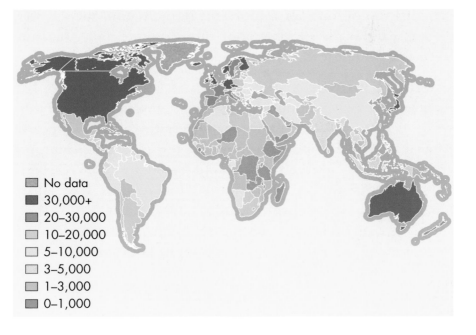

- No data
- 30,000+
- 20–30,000
- 10–20,000
- 5–10,000
- 3–5,000
- 1–3,000
- 0–1,000

Highest GDP and highest GDP per capita 2014

Country	Total national GDP (US$millions)	Country	GDP per capita (US$)
World	74,899,882	World	10,513
United States	16,912,540	Luxembourg	112,404
China	9,925,540	Norway	106,134
Japan	6,162,510	Qatar	98,857
Germany	3,462,000	Switzerland	81,284
Brazil	2,985,310	Australia	69,674

Lower GDP nations

Tuvalu's GDP is cited as the world's lowest (US$40 million). The lowest per capita (i.e. per person) rate is in Burundi (US$251). In terms of GDP per capita, it is no great surprise that the countries with the lowest levels are mostly in sub-Saharan Africa, along with a few Asian countries like Afghanistan, Burma and Nepal. These poor results reflect a combination of long-term problems in the region such as war, disease, natural catastrophe, poor infrastructure and education levels and widespread corruption.

Economic growth

In recent years economists have seen a major change in the world economy. While traditionally wealthy areas like North America and Europe continue to prosper, the emerging economies of southern Asia are becoming increasingly important. As well as historically rich nations like Japan, Singapore and South Korea, the likes of India and China are now flying up the economic charts. Apart from the advantage of a massive labour supply, both countries have become centres of cutting-edge technology. Because the start-up costs and wages are low compared to most developed nations, more and more businesses are turning to the East.

Most nations in sub-Saharan Africa have poor or even negative economic growth, although Equatorial Guinea has notably defied this trend with a growth rate of almost 26 per cent between 1993 and 2003 – the highest in the world over that time period thanks to an oil boom.

Currency and exchange rates

Currency is the monetary unit of exchange in a country or region – like the dollar, the pound or the rupee. Most countries have their own currency under the control of their national government but there are exceptions, such as those countries in the European Union who have adopted the euro and handed over control of monetary policy to the European Central Bank.

The exchange rate indicates how much one country's currency is worth against that of another country. For instance, the exchange rate between the United Kingdom and the United States means that one pound sterling will buy you about US$1.75, though this is constantly fluctuating. Most people's experience with exchange rates is limited to vacations abroad, but differences in exchange rates have profound effects on global business and massive fortunes are won and lost on the foreign exchange markets.

The Big Mac Index

The Big Mac Index was introduced by *The Economist* magazine in the mid-1980s. It uses a system called "Burgernomics," based on how much a McDonald's Big Mac costs in the 120 countries where it is available. "Burgernomics" works on the theory of purchasing power parity (PPP), the idea that a dollar should buy you the same amount regardless of where you are in the world.

Theoretically, exchange rates between two countries should move towards the rate where things cost the same in both countries. The Big Mac PPP is the exchange rate at which hamburgers cost the same in the United States as abroad. Comparing the Big Mac PPP with the actual exchange rate then suggests if a currency is under- or overvalued. *The Economist* has developed a similar index using Starbucks coffee – the "Tall Latte" index!

International trade

The first long-distance trade was probably between buyers and sellers from Mesopotamia and the Indus Valley sometime around 3000 BCE, while the Phoenicians later became important maritime traders throughout the Mediterranean. For around 2,000 years starting from 500 BCE, the "Silk Road" – a network covering around 4,000 miles – was the main route for trade in goods like silk and spices between

ABOVE Thousands of shipping containers awaiting delivery in Hong Kong.

China, India, Europe and the Near East. The stability of the Roman Empire also helped trade during this time, and its collapse was to have an impact for several centuries.

• Between the fifteenth and seventeenth centuries, the major European nations set about trying to find profitable new trade routes around the world, relying on maritime routes instead of overland transport to bring about the Age of Discovery. During this period, some parts of the world were governed by trading organisations such as the British East India Company.

• When international merchant trade first began to boom in the sixteenth and seventeenth centuries, some of the most important products were slaves and spices. Later, woven cotton became a major commodity, as did opium.

• In the late nineteenth century, many trading nations adopted the "gold standard," meaning that their currencies were guaranteed to be exchangeable for gold. While once considered to be the economic foundation of international trade, this system was discarded by 1931, and is blamed by some for the Great Depression.

A country's total exports minus its imports is called the balance of payments and is one of the most important indicators of a nation's trading health. A trade surplus (where exports outstrip imports) is seen as a generally good thing but many thriving economies run a deficit and economists increasingly argue that this is not a bad thing. However, unredeemed deficits in a country's balance of payments will lead to foreign debt.

Foreign debt

Foreign debt is the money a government owes to creditors abroad, which can include banks, other governments or international financial bodies like the World Bank or the International Monetary Fund. Third World debt – foreign debt accumulated by developing nations – is a major international issue and there is a growing movement demanding that rich developed nations cancel the debt still owed by the Third World. This movement argues that some countries have to pay back so much debt to the developed world that they have no chance of developing their own economies, leading to a spiral of further poverty and more borrowing.

"Debt burden" refers to how much a country's foreign debt amounts to as a proportion of their GDP.

Highest debt and highest debt burden

Country	Debt (US$million; 2012)	Country	Debt (% GDP; 2012)
United States	15,940,978	Japan	230
United Kingdom	9,307,090	Greece	163
Germany	5,539,282	Jamaica	139
France	5,303,543	Lebanon	126
Japan	2,826,649	Eritrea	134

Foreign aid

Many countries, especially those in the developed world, have foreign aid programmes offering economic help and advice to poorer nations. This aid is usually in one of three forms: long-term aid to support economic development; short-term aid to help in the aftermath of a humanitarian crisis; or military aid to help a country with internal or external defence problems.

The world's biggest donor nations are those with the biggest economies: the United States, followed by Japan, France, Germany and the United Kingdom. Between them, these nations give around $50 billion annually. The biggest recipients of this aid are the Democratic Republic of Congo, Iraq, Vietnam, Indonesia and Tanzania.

FACT
In June 2005, finance ministers from the world's most powerful developed economies made the landmark decision to cancel US$40 billion worth of debt owed to the World Bank, thus bringing economic relief to 18 of the world's poorest countries.

International economic organisations

Since the Second World War, a number of international organisations have been established to deal with economic issues from a global perspective.

The World Bank

The World Bank is made up of two institutions owned by the 188 member countries: the International Bank for Reconstruction and Development, and the International Development Association. It is an agency of the United Nations and has operated since 1946 with the aim of providing funding and advice to the poorest members of the UN so that they can develop their economies and reduce poverty. The Bank raises its funds through annual contributions from member nations and through its activities on the world's financial markets. In 2014, it had an expenditure of nearly US$35 billion, supporting 1,260 projects in 100 countries.

To help with analysis and to decide on the best way to implement programmes, the Bank puts countries into one of four groupings according to their per capita income. In 2013 these were: low income ($1,035 or less); lower middle income (between $1,036 and $4,085); upper middle income (between $4,086 and $12,615); and high income ($12,616 or more). It has resident missions in 64 developing nations and runs regional offices for East and West Africa, the Baltic States and south-east Asia to help with UN development projects.

The International Monetary Fund

The International Monetary Fund (IMF) is an international organisation designed to oversee global economic affairs, including developing sustainable economic growth and reducing poverty. It does this mainly by monitoring exchange rates and balance of payments and by providing advice and financial help to countries having problems with their balance of payments. The IMF, which began its work in 1947 and now includes 188 member states, works in co-operation with the United Nations.

ABOVE A G8 meeting hosted by Russia in March 2006.

G8

The G8 (an abbreviation for "Group of Eight") is an informal alliance of major industrial nations that meets to discuss major international problems and ways to overcome them. It was set up in the mid-1970s in response to a world economic recession following the 1973 oil crisis, and the original members were France, Germany, Italy, Japan, the United Kingdom and the United States. Canada and Russia have since joined to make up the '8', while the EU has an observer status.

The G8 has many critics though and has been accused of being an unofficial "world government" looking out for the interests of rich nations. Since the late 1990s, large-scale anti-globalisation protests have run alongside the talks, often ending in violence.

FACT

Just before the G8 summit of 2005, a series of 10 concerts were held throughout the world to bring attention to the issue of Third World debt. The concerts had a live audience of 1 million people, the largest, simultaneous rock concert attendance ever. It also had one of the largest ever TV audiences, estimated at between 2 and 3 billion.

Natural resources

Natural resources can bring great wealth and international importance to a country but economies can become over-reliant on them and thus find themselves economically vulnerable if a particular resource runs out, is spoilt or suffers drastic price decreases in the international market. Many of the world's leading economies are conspicuously non-reliant on natural resources for their wealth, relying instead on infrastructural capital and technological expertise. Obtaining and processing natural resources can have serious environmental effects which many governments have only recently started to take seriously.

There are two major types of natural resource. The first type is renewable resources, ones which restock themselves as they are harvested, like coffee or fish. Non-renewable resources have finite supplies and include old-growth forests, oil, coal, gas and other minerals.

ABOVE Freshly cut timber, ready for processing.

Oil

Increasing industrialisation has made oil one of the most important traded natural resources in the world, and its discovery in the Middle East in the twentieth century created many super-rich states. It also increased political tensions in the region, and gave foreign governments a strong motivation for political or military intervention. The United States is by far the world's biggest oil consumer, followed by Japan, China, Russia and Germany.

ABOVE An oil rig in the Atlantic Ocean.

Highest oil consumers and producers 2011

Top oil producers	(million barrels per day)	Top oil consumers	(million barrels per day)
Russia	10.12	United States	18.84
Saudi Arabia	9.76	China	9.79
United States	9.06	Japan	4.46
Iran	3.99	India	3.29
China	4.07	Russia	3.20

These figures include crude oil, natural gas liquids, condensate, refinery gain and other liquids.

FACT

The world uses about 30 billion barrels of oil per year.

Timber

Timber has been traded for centuries but over-consumption has devastating effects on the environment and deforestation poses a serious threat to our ecosystem. Today, wood is used for a huge number of purposes – from fuel to construction to making paper. The world's top timber producer is the United States, followed by India, China, Brazil and Canada.

Coffee

Coffee is among the most widely traded commodities in the world and is particularly important to the economies of many developing countries, accounting for as much as 80 per cent of foreign exchange earnings. Brazil is the biggest producer, accounting for over 26 per cent of the 7.2 million tons harvested worldwide in 2001. Vietnam is next biggest, producing 12 per cent of the total, while Colombia produces around 11 per cent.

LEFT The world's increasing coffee "addiction" has seen the commodity become one of the world's most valuable cash crops.

FACT

A US coin, the 1933 Double Eagle, was auctioned in New York in 2002 for US$7.59 million. The value of the coin when it was first issued was US$20. That's inflation for you…

Gold

South Africa is the world's biggest producer of gold, with 308.4 tonnes mined in 2004. It has been the main global supplier since the nineteenth century and in 1970, accounted for almost 80 per cent of production. The next biggest producers are the United States (282.3 tonnes), Australia (280.1 tonnes), China (211 tonnes) and Russia (180.5 tonnes).

ABOVE Gold ingots from the Bank of Sweden.

Diamonds

Because they are valuable, easy to transport and difficult to trace, diamonds have been used to fund militias in wars throughout West Africa in recent years, especially in Angola, the Congo, Liberia and Sierra Leone. Botswana, however, has managed to avoid this pitfall and is now the world's biggest diamond producer by value, using the income to develop its economy. Russia is the next biggest producer and Australia, the Democratic Republic of Congo and South Africa are also important players.

FACT

The world's most expensive diamond was the 100-carat Star of the Season, which was sold in Geneva, Switzerland for US$16,548,750 in 1995. The largest diamond was the Cullinan diamond, mined in South Africa in 1905. It was five inches across and 3,106 carats. It was cut into 105 separate jewels, including the 530 carat Star of Africa, some of which are now in the British Crown Jewels.

Industry

Most of the world's most prosperous nations are industrialised – they have highly developed industries where workers are brought together and organised so they work efficiently and have the best chance of creating profit.

For much of human history people worked on a small scale, often in agriculture, with the aim of producing just enough for themselves and their family or extended social group. About four-fifths of Europe lived like this in medieval days and many people in the developing world continue to do so. However, Europe underwent an Industrial Revolution in the eighteenth and nineteenth centuries, when developments in technology (like steam power and the invention of automatic weaving machines) meant production could take place on a much larger scale than before. Life changed dramatically as people began to work in huge factories and machines took over from manual labour. The effects of the Industrial Revolution soon spread to North America and to the corners of the world then under European control. A second Industrial Revolution stretched into the twentieth century as electricity and the internal combustion engine altered the way we worked again.

ABOVE While textiles were one of the first products to be fully industrialised in the Europe, these workers in Maharashta, India, still process raw cotton by hand.

FACT

Richard Arkwright (1732-92) was one of the key figures in the Industrial Revolution. He understood the profits to be made from carrying out all the stages of production in a single place. Arkwright converted the British textile industry from cottage production into a business organised around large mills or factories. He died a very rich man.

During the twentieth century, many less developed countries became industrialised under the influence of the United States and the Soviet Union. Not all of these industrialisation programmes were successful, as some countries lacked the mature economic basis and responsible governance required to compete in the free market. Today, there are several countries classified as Newly Industrialising Countries – not quite yet up to the industrial levels of developed nations, but getting there. Modern NICs include China and India, Malaysia, the Philippines, Thailand, Mexico, Turkey and several of the Persian Gulf states.

Reasearch and Development

For modern industrialised nations, research and development (R&D) is one of the most important ways of keeping ahead of the game. R&D is usually carried out by specialised organisations run by governments, companies or universities, to develop new technologies which can ultimately be used for commercial benefit.

The country in the world that spends most on R&D is Israel, where 4.66 per cent of the GDP is dedicated to technological development. The next highest spenders are Sweden, Finland, Japan and Iceland, all spending more than 3 per cent of their GDPs on R&D. A typical large industrial company might spend about 3 per cent of its revenue on R&D, while a computing company might expect to spend around 7 per cent.

The working world

Labour

In 2011, there were 3 billion workers around the world, a little over 61 per cent of the world's population between the ages of 15 and 64. Almost a fifth of the total global workforce is based in China. The single biggest employer in the world is the US Department of Defense, which provides work for 3.2 million people. The biggest private employer is the American retailer Wal-Mart, which employs around 2.1 million.

Most occupations fit into one of three broad groups: agriculture, industry and services. Below is a pie chart showing how the world's workers are divided between these sectors:

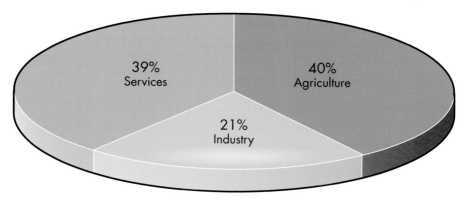

The International Labour Organization (ILO) estimates that almost 1.3 billion workers earned less than $1.25 a day in 2011, and almost 2.4 billion earned less than two dollars. Unemployment across the globe is just under 8.4 per cent.

Child workers

Child labour is a serious problem in many parts of the developing world, with children often expected to do dangerous and tiring jobs for very low wages and at the expense of their education. It is estimated that 30 per cent of 10–14 year olds in Africa have to work, as do 20 per cent in Asia. Mali has the highest child worker rate in the world, with over 51 per cent of 10–14 year olds in employment.

Big business

Stock exchanges

Every day massive volumes of stocks, shares and other securities are bought and sold at exchanges throughout the world. These transactions are vital to the world's economies and create funds to invest in new business ventures while offering investors the chance to share in the profits.

Brokers, the people whose job it is to actually trade securities, first emerged in twelfth-century France as representatives of banks who traded agricultural debts with each other. A century later, traders from Bruges in Belgium met to trade commodities in a house belonging to a man named van der Burse, and to this day there are

ABOVE The Frankfurt Stock Exchange is among the world's busiest.

many exchanges around Europe called Bourses. Trading in debts and securities was commonplace throughout Europe but mostly done unofficially, often in coffee houses. The first official stock exchange was set up in Antwerp, Belgium in 1460. The first ever official share issue by a company was in Amsterdam in the early seventeenth century when shares were offered in the Dutch East India Company.

For a long time, exchanges were unregulated and financial scandals were regularly discovered, but over the years they have adopted complex rules designed to protect buyers and sellers. A large proportion of trading now takes place across computer connections rather than in physical places.

The world's biggest exchanges in terms of market capitalisation are New York, Tokyo, NASDAQ (an American electronic market), London and Euronext (created by the merger of exchanges in Belgium, France, the Netherlands, Portugal and the United Kingdom).

Entrepreneurs

Entrepreneurs are the heroes of capitalism, the people who can make outrageous fortunes with a great idea, driving ambition or the ability to convince others to join them. Bill Gates, Chairman and Chief Software Architect of the Microsoft Corporation, is the world's most successful entrepreneur. His personal fortune is bigger than the GDP of all but the 60 or so largest economies in the world, though he is also famous for his enormous contributions to philanthropic causes.

World's richest people

Name	Nationality	Source	Estimated net worth (US$billion)
Bill Gates	American	Information technology	79.4
Carlos Slim Helu	Mexican	Telecommunications	79
Warren Buffett	American	Investments	62.2
Amancio Ortega	Spanish	Retailing	60.7
Larry Ellison	American	Information technology	49.3

Biggest companies

The Forbes Global 2000 is compiled by *Forbes Magazine* and ranks the world's 2,000 most successful public companies, judging them on their sales, profit, assets and market value. In 2014, three of the top five companies were Chinese. The biggest was the Industrial and Commercial Bank of China, followed by China Construction Bank and the Agricultural Bank of China. JPMorgan Chase bank group, based in the United States, came next. The rest of the top 10, in descending order, were: Berkshire Hathaway (United States; investment services), Exxon Mobil (United States; oil and gas), General Electric (United States; conglomerate), Wells Fargo (United States; banking), Bank of China (China; banking) and PetroChina (China; oil and gas).

ABOVE On 24 March 1989, Exxon were responsible for one of the world's worst environmental disasters, contaminating over 2,000 km (1,200 miles) of the Alaskan shoreline with oil spilt from one of their tankers.

Global brands

Interbrand/Business Week runs a list similar to the Forbes 2000, except that it looks at the value of individual brands rather than whole companies which might own several brands. The United States dominates this list, as home to 9 of the 10 most valuable global brands. The most valuable is, not surprisingly, Apple, worth an estimated US$87.3 billion. Samsung Group (based in South Korea) is second, valued at US$58.7 billion. The companies making up the rest of the top 10 are Google, Microsoft, Verizon, General Electric, AT&T, Amazon.com, Walmart and IBM.

A fair deal

Transparency International (TI) is an organisation that aims to highlight business corruption throughout the world. Its analysis is based on the definition of corruption as the abuse of public office for private gain. TI creates its list by analysing results from confidential polls around the world and they do acknowledge that what might be seen as corruption in one country may be viewed as a legitimate business practice in another. However, they do try to set some standard of internationally acceptable behaviour. Out of 159 countries rated by TI, those that get the best marks are mostly Scandinavian – Iceland, Finland and Denmark – with New Zealand and Singapore also making up the top five. The most corrupt countries in the world were found to be Haiti, Myanmar, Turkmenistan, Bangladesh and Chad.

FACT
The world's biggest and most notorious case of corporate corruption was that of Enron, an energy company based in Texas. The revelation of fraudulent practices in late 2001 caused the share price to drop from $90 to $0.30, costing shareholders millions of dollars.

CITIES,
TRANSPORT AND
COMMUNICATIONS

Urban planning

With so many people in such a small area, cities pose particularly difficult problems for planners. Some cities, like London and Paris, have grown organically over the course of many centuries and are largely unplanned. Others have been laid out to a very definite scheme, most often on a grid pattern. The radial scheme, with a central square joined to a series of concentric outer-roads, has also been popular. Archaeologists argue about what the oldest planned city was, but the remains of Mohenjo-daro (in modern day Pakistan) reveal a grid-plan city built 4,000–5,000 years ago by the Indus Valley civilisation.

Skyscrapers

Skyscrapers are the defining image of the modern city. Listed below are the top five tallest in the world:

Building	Location	Year completed	Height feet	Height meters
Burj Khalifa	Dubai	2010	2,717	828
Shanghai Tower	Shanghai	2014	2,073	632
Makkah Royal Clock Tower Hotel	Mecca	2012	1,971	601
One World Trade Center	New York City	2014	1,776	541.3
Taipei 101	Taipei	2004	1,669	509

FACT

Toronto, Canada, has overcome its shortage of space by building the largest underground shopping complex on the planet. The PATH Walkway covers 27 km (16 miles) of shopping arcades and has 371,600 square metres (4 million sq ft) of retail space.

Railways

The first public railway was a horse-drawn service in south London called the Surrey Iron Railway, which opened in 1803. The following year a Welshman, Richard Trevithick, succeeded in building a railway steam locomotive, which led to the opening of the first permanent steam railway (the Stockton and Darlington Railway in England) in 1825. Below are the world's five longest networks today:

Location	Distance km	Distance miles
United States	227,736	141,515
Russia	87,157	54,157
China	70,898	44,677
India	63,230	39,291
Canada	48,683	30,252

ABOVE French TGV trains (*Train à Grande Vitesse*) have been in operation since 1981. They travel at up to 320 km/h (200 mph), with a passenger network that now reaches beyond France into Belgium, Switzerland, Italy, the Netherlands, Germany and England.

Underground urban networks

The first underground rail network in the world was built in London in 1863, at a time when it was the biggest city in the world. London's is still the biggest urban underground rail system, with 390 kilometres of track, and now carrying over 2.5 million people every day. The next two underground train systems to be built were in Paris (1900) and New York (1904), with New York evolving to have more stations than any other: 486. The two other biggest underground rail systems are in Tokyo (opened 1927) and Moscow (1935).

FACT
In 2004, Geoff Marshall and Neil Blake managed to visit every one of the stations on the London Underground in a record 18 hours, 35 minutes and 43 seconds. They finished so late that they missed their last train home and had to take a taxi.

Highways

Humans have been engineering roads for almost 6,000 years as a way of getting people more efficiently from one place to another, be it on foot, on horseback or in carts and wagons. It was the age of the car, however, that inspired a road-building boom as never seen before. The United States has the biggest road network on the planet, with almost 6.4 million kilometres (4 million miles) of roads. Next comes China, followed by Canada, India and Brazil.

Japan produces the most cars in the world, estimated at between 8.5 and 9 million a year. Germany and the United States are the next biggest manufacturers. America's General Motors is the largest motor vehicle company and manufactures over 8 million motor vehicles every year.

FACT

The longest continuous road in the world is the Pan-American Highway, which covers 25,750 kilometres (16,000 miles) from Alaska to Brazil and passes through 12 different countries. The longest street – though most of it exists as Highway 11 – is Yonge Street, which starts in Toronto and stretches for 1,896 kilometres (1,178 miles).

ABOVE Night-time traffic around the industrial port of Ludwigshafen, Germany.

FACT

The Himalayan kingdom of Bhutan has no traffic lights – they were removed in the late 1990s for being eyesores.

Bridges and tunnels

Seas, rivers, hills and valleys all create formidable natural barriers to human transport, leading us to develop bridges and tunnels to get over, through or under. The first known "engineered" bridge, an arch bridge that still stands in Turkey, dates back to around 850 BCE. The Romans took bridge-building to another level, using bricks and mortar to build vast arch bridges and aqueducts. The Industrial Revolution brought about the next great revolution in bridges, as iron, and later steel, were used, allowing for far more complex designs such as the suspension bridge.

The world's current largest bridges are listed below:

Bridge	Location	Year completed	Span in metres	Span in feet
Danyang–Kunshan Grand Bridge	China	2010	164,800	540,700
Tianjin Grand Bridge	China	2010	113,700	373,000
Weinan Weihe Grand Bridge	China	2008	79,732	261,588
Bang Na Expressway	Thailand	2000	54,000	177,000
Beijing Grand Bridge	China	2010	48,153	157,982

As well as "going over," the Romans were the early masters of "going under," using complex systems of aqueducts and tunnels to transport water. Tunnels were also important components in canal networks, but it was with the emergence of the train and the motorcar that tunnel-building came into its own. Today, engineers are building tunnels that are ever longer and deeper, such as the Seikan tunnel in Japan, opened in 1988, which is just over 51.5 kilometres (32 miles) in length. The AlpTransit Link, cutting a quicker train route under the Alps from Switzerland to Italy, is planned to be even longer at 57 kilometres (35.4 miles), though it is not expected to be completed until about 2015. The next longest tunnel in the world is the Channel Tunnel, completed in 1994, which runs underneath the English Channel between France and England, a distance of 50 kilometres (31 miles).

Waterways

A waterway is defined as any navigable stretch of inland water, including seas, lakes, rivers and canals. Canals are manmade waterways, the earliest of which was built by the Mesopotamians around 4000 BCE. The world's longest canal is the Grand Canal in China, which extends 1,795 kilometres (1,114 miles). It is three times longer than the 6th biggest, the Erie Canal in New York (584 kilometres or 363 miles). As technology has progressed, the boats that we use to navigate across long stretches of water have gradually got bigger. Here are some of the largest now in existence:

Largest container ship – *the Magleby Maersk (launched in 2013) weighs in at 174,500 tonnes, making it the biggest sailing vessel of any kind.*

Largest aircraft carrier – *the Nimitz class US Navy aircraft carriers have a full load displacement of approximately 97,000 long tonnes. In 2015, the Gerald R. Ford class supercarriers will become the largest in the world with a full load displacement of approximately 100,000 tonnes.*

Largest car ferry – *Irish Ferries" Ulysses (launched in 2000) can carry 1,342 cars.*

ABOVE The Nimitz class aircraft carrier *John C. Stennis*, at Pearl Harbor, Hawaii.

Largest passenger liner – *The Oasis class ships, the* Oasis of the Seas *and* Allure of the Seas *(launched in 2009), are 1,181 feet (360 meters) long and 154 feet (47 meters) wide. They have room for over 5,400 passengers and and almost half as many crew.*

Largest yacht – Azzam, *a yacht rumored to be owned by a powerful Middle Eastern billionaire, is 590 feet (180 meters) long and launched in 2013.*

FACT

Egypt's Suez Canal is the world's seventh largest canal and one of the most strategically important. Egyptian leader Abdul Nasser became a national hero when he nationalised the canal in 1956, despite military threats from Britain and France, both of which held shares in its foreign ownership.

ABOVE The *Queen Mary 2* on the Elbe River near Kollmar in Germany. The *Queen Mary 2* is Cunard's flagship and one of the largest passenger ships in the world.

ABOVE Hong Kong's port from space. The small yellow dots in the water are ships.

Ports

Ports are one of the most ancient and enduring images of urban civilisation. Ports have been busy centres of commerce for as long as the sea has been used as a means of trade, and have traditionally been more cosmopolitan and diverse than inland cities. Hong Kong is now the world's biggest port, handling over 20 million TEU per year. The next biggest is Singapore, and the rest of the top five – Shanghai, Shenzen and Busan – are all in south-east Asia. The two biggest non-Asian ports are Los Angeles, and Rotterdam in the Netherlands.

FACT
The oldest working port in the world is almost certainly Jaffa in Israel, which has a history that can be traced back 4,000 years. According to the Old Testament, it was from here that Jonah began the voyage on which he was swallowed by a whale.

Air travel

Air travel was largely invented in the first half of the twentieth century, and has quickly grown to become a fairly standard mode of transport, at least in the wealthier parts of the world. The number of people travelling by plane has increased sharply in recent decades, and while this certainly helps to bring the world closer together, it has also brought into focus the environmental impact of aviation. The busiest airports in the world are Atlanta's Hartsfield International, Chicago's O"Hare, London's Heathrow and Haneda airport in Tokyo.

Landmarks in the history of aviation

YEAR	EVENT
1487	Leonardo da Vinci designs a flying machine which he never tests.
1670	Francesco de Lana designs an airship.
1783	The Montgolfier Brothers" hot air balloon rises to a height of 2,000 metres (6,560 feet).
1785	Jean Blanchard and John Jeffries cross the English Channel in a balloon.
1853	Triplane designed by George Cayley successfully flies 275 m (900 feet).
1900	Count Ferdinand von Zeppelin's airship makes its first flight.
1903	The Wright Brothers fly the first heavier-than-air machine at Kitty Hawk, United States.
1909	Louis Bleriot makes first heavier-than-air machine flight across the English Channel.
1912	Count von Zeppelin establishes first commercial airline.
1916	First heavy bomber, the Handley Page, used in battle.
1927	Charles Lindbergh becomes first person to cross the Atlantic non-stop.
1932	Amelia Earhart becomes first woman pilot to cross the Atlantic.
1936	The Spitfire and the Messerschmitt 110 make their first flights.
1937	Frank Whittle tests a prototype jet engine.
1947	Test pilot Chuck Yeager breaks the sound barrier.
1971	The Boeing 747 travels from New York to London on its maiden commercial flight.
1976	Concorde, the first supersonic commercial airliner, goes into service.
2003	On the centenary of the Wright Brothers' flight, Concorde is withdrawn from service.

Space flight

The intense rivalry between the Soviet Union and the United States in the twentieth century inspired the "space race" that saw dramatic advances in human space exploration. The two events that most captured the human imagination both occurred in the 1960s. On 12 April 1961 the Soviets sent a man into orbit for the first time, making Yuri Gagarin and his *Vostok I* household names. Then on 21 July 1969 two Americans, Neil Armstrong and Buzz Aldrin, became the first men to step on the Moon when they left *Apollo 11*. Today, the most important space agencies are NASA, the European Space Agency (ESA) and those of China and Russia.

Above Buzz Aldrin, as photographed by Neil Armstrong on the Moon, July 1969.

ABOVE Aerial view of *Apollo 11* on its transporter, 1969.

Landmarks in space exploration

The Soviet Union/Russia has the most space experience with over 17,200 man days in space. The United States has just over 9,800 days.

The Apollo 13 crew of James Lovell, Fred Haise, and John Swigert have gone further from the Earth than anyone else. Their trip to the far side of the Moon on 15 April 1970 took them 400,171 kilometres (248,655 miles) away from our planet.

Two Americans hold the record for the most space flights. Franklin Chang-Diaz made seven missions between 1986 and 2002 and Jerry Ross made the same number between 1985 and 2002.

The Russian, Sergei Krikalev, has spent the most time in space – a total of 803 days, 9 hours and 39 minutes.

Vladimír Remek of Czechoslovakia was the first person from outside the United States and the Soviet Union to go into space, on the Soviet-run Soyuz 28 mission in March 1978.

Valentina Tereshkova of the Soviet Union was the first woman to go into space, in the Vostok 6 *mission of 1963.*

Laika, a stray dog from the streets of Moscow, was the first dog sent into space orbit, aboard the Soviet Sputnik 2 *in 1957. Unfortunately, she died when the cabin over-heated four days after take-off.*

James Voss and Susan Helms undertook the longest ever spacewalk when they left their NASA space shuttle for 8 hours, 56 minutes on 11 March 2001.

The first joint American-Soviet space programme was the Apollo-Soyuz *Test Project in July 1975.*

The International Space Station

The International Space Station (ISS) has allowed a permanent human presence in space since it went into orbit on 20 November 1998. It is still being built, but has room for six crew members to carry out experiments to increase our understanding of space. The station is serviced by the American space shuttle and the Russian *Soyuz* and *Progress* spacecraft units. All the main expedition crews have been from the United States or Russia, but the station has had visitors from all over the world, including several paying "space tourists."

The station is jointly run by NASA, the Russian Federal Space Agency, the ESA, the Canadian Space Agency and the National Space Agency of Japan. It orbits at around 360 kilometres (220 miles) above the Earth at an average speed of 27,685.7 km/h – taking just over an hour and a half to orbit the earth.

Telecommunications

When Alexander Graham Bell patented the first telephone in 1876, he could have had little idea just how important it would become in our lives. In 2005, it was estimated that sales of mobile ringtones alone had reached US$600 million, around twice as much as they earned in 2004.

FACT
The Burj Khalifa Skyscraper in Dubai, United Arab Emirates, built in 2010, is the world's largest free-standing structure, measuring 2,722 feet (829.8 meters).

Mobile phones per 100 people

Country	Number of mobile phones
Hong Kong	239
Gabon	215
Kuwait	190
Kazakhstan	181
Maldives	181

Internet hosts and computers

Whether it's staying in touch, playing games or surfing the net, people are spending more time than ever at their computers. People spend the most time on computers (outside work hours) in Canada, where the average is 43.5 hours per month. Americans average 35.3 hours per month, while the British average 32.3.

In the last 10 years, the Internet has revolutionised the way we access information across the world. Sir Tim Berners-Lee is regarded as the father of the "World Wide Web." In the late 1980s and early 1990s, he created a hypertext language that allowed academics to share information over a computer network, the basis of the system still used by the net. He is now the head of the World Wide Web Consortium in Boston.

America has the most websites in the top one million of any country, hosting over 431,000 in 2012. Germany has the next highest number, but with 82,000, it is five times fewer than the United States.

Radio and television

Television and radio emerged from the work of many different scientists at the end of the nineteenth and beginning of the twentieth centuries. The invention of the radio as we know it – or "wireless" as it was then known – is usually credited to the Italian Guglielmo Marconi, who was awarded the world's first patent for radio in 1896 and opened up a wireless factory in England two years later.

In 1925, a Scotsman, John Logie Baird, demonstrated the first television transmission – a slightly fuzzy image of a ventriloquist dummy's head. Within two years the Bell Telephone Corporation broadcast the first long-range images, between New York and Washington, DC. In 1936, 10 years after Logie Baird's first demonstration of TV, there were still only about 200 television sets around the world but by 1996, this had increased to 1 billion and grows day by day. Since those images of the dummy's head, television has given us the chance to share in many great events like man's first step on the Moon, the collapse of the Berlin Wall and Nelson Mandela's release from prison.

The citizens of Thailand are the biggest television addicts, watching an average of 22.4 hours per week, followed by the Philippines (21 hours) and Egypt (20.9 hours). Listening to the radio is most popular in Argentina, where citizens spend an average 20.8 hours a week tuned in. The next biggest listeners are in neighbouring Brazil (17.2 hours) and South Africa (15.0 hours).

FACT

Baywatch is the most watched TV series in history, reaching an average 1.1 billion audience in 142 countries per week at its peak in 1996. That figure, though, is dwarfed by the 2.5 billion who watched Princess Diana's funeral in 1997, and the estimated 2–3 billion who watched the Live 8 concerts in 2005.

Media

The Nordic countries are the biggest newspaper readers in the world, with Iceland, Norway, Sweden and Finland making up four of the top five. The other nation in the top five is Japan, which is home to the biggest-selling daily paper, *Yomiuri Shimbun*, with a circulation of over 14 million. The biggest-circulation English language paper is the United Kingdom's *The Sun*, with an average 3.5 million readers.

Freedom of the press

Reporters without Boundaries produces an annual index of press freedom throughout the world. The index takes into account factors such as pressures exerted on journalists by government and non-government organisations. The index is, by its nature, based on "unofficial" data, and so rankings are inevitably subjective. Nonetheless, the index is a tool widely used by organisations concerned with freedom of speech. All of the top ten most free nations are European, with seven countries ranked equally in first place. They are: Finland, Iceland, Norway, Netherlands, Denmark, Switzerland and Ireland. The lowest ranked countries (in descending order) are Vietnam, China, Nepal, Cuba, Libya, Myanmar, Iran, Turkmenistan, Eritrea and North Korea.

FACT

In 1983, the famous German magazine, *Stern*, fell for one of the biggest hoaxes of all time when it paid US$6 million for what were apparently 60 volumes of Hitler's diaries. They were revealed as forgeries within a few weeks, but not before several other newspapers and magazines around the world had fallen foul of the fraud.

HUMAN
ACHIEVEMENT

Expanding our horizons

Human civilisation is always looking to better itself – to explore the limits of endeavour, achievement and ingenuity. Sometimes this is a test of the individual but often it has been for the glory of a larger social group and sometimes even for the greater good of all humankind.

The oldest civilisation

We know of ancient civilisations in Mesopotamia (present day Iraq), Egypt and the Indus Valley dating back to around 10,000 BCE, but which died out over time. The oldest civilization still alive today is China, tracing its roots back to at least 2500 BCE. When we talk of civilisation, we mean the region has certain defining characteristics like a recorded language system and skills, in particular arts and crafts. It was also higly developed in terms of agriculture and technology and had a comparatively centralised system of administration and law. These elements did not suddenly emerge over the whole region at the same time, but rather evolved throughout the geographical area over a long period.

ABOVE Part of the Great Wall of China, which dates back to the third century BCE.

Military conquerors
Alexander the Great
(Greece; 356–323 BCE)
The King of Macedon from 336–323 BCE. In his short life, Alexander came closer than anyone to conquering all of the known world. He inherited a united Greece and then conquered the Persian Empire and extended his rule as far as the Punjab.

Alexander the Great

Genghis Khan
(Mongolia; c.1162–1227)
The feared and respected founder of the Mongol Empire, which united the disparate peoples of Central Asia. He extended his empire to include parts of northern China, Turkistan, Transoxania and Afghanistan. He also led raiding missions into Persia and Europe, as far as the Dnieper River. His dynasty lasted for centuries and he is still regarded as "father of the nation" in Mongolia, despite his reputation for brutality.

Genghis Khan

Napoleon Bonaparte
(France; 1769–1821)
Bonaparte was a military genius who crowned himself Emperor of France, having conquered lands from Portugal to Italy and north to the River Elbe. His plans for European domination ended only with a disastrous defeat in Moscow in 1812 and, finally, against the Duke of Wellington at Waterloo (in Belgium) three years later. His tactics continue to be studied today.

Napoleon Bonaparte

The biggest empire

The British Empire encompassed more territory and people than any other empire in the history of the world. It started to emerge at the end of the fifteenth century as Europe entered into its golden age of discovery and colonisation. It reached its peak in the late nineteenth and early twentieth centuries, covering over 36.4 million square kilometres (14 million sq miles) and including one quarter of the world's population. At various stages it included lands throughout Africa, Asia, the Pacific and North America. The empire crumbled in the twentieth century in the face of two World Wars and the rise of independence movements, though many former colonies went on to join the Commonwealth.

Five great explorers

Marco Polo (Italy; 1254–1324)

According to his own book, *The Travels of Marco Polo*, he, his father and uncle travelled to China (then known as Cathay) via the Silk Road and spent years at the court of the Mongol emperor, Kublai Khan. He was responsible for introducing Europeans to the East and inspired future European voyages of discovery, though historians have since cast doubt on the truth of some of his accounts.

Admiral Zheng He (China; 1371–1433)

Zheng made seven voyages to the Indian Ocean between 1405 and 1433, covering 56,315 kilometres (35,000 miles) and traveling to 30 different Asian and African countries. He introduced Chinese civilisation to vast new areas of the world and was famed for a fleet of massive ships – some perhaps as long as 120 metres (400 feet).

Christopher Columbus (Italian; 1451–1506)

Flying under the Spanish flag in 1492, Columbus" proposed voyage to India actually resulted in his discovery of America. Although the Vikings got there several centuries earlier, it was his discovery that gave momentum to European settlement and thus the Americas as we know them today.

Ferdinand Magellan (Portugal; 1480–1521)

Magellan set sail under the Spanish flag in 1519 in search of a route to the Spice Islands via the west side of South America. He is credited as the first person to circumnavigate the world, though he died before the voyage finally docked back in Spain in 1521, killed in a dispute at Mactan in the Philippines. Of the five ships and 250 men who left in 1519, only one ship and 18 men made it home.

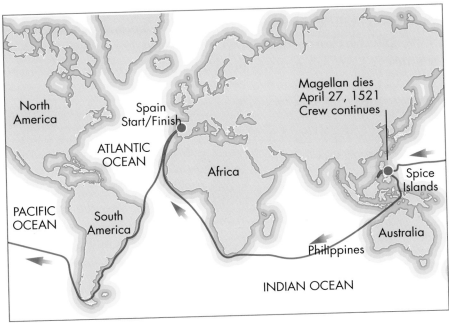

ABOVE The first voyage around the world, led by Ferdinand Magellan.

James Cook (Great Britain; 1728–1779)

Cook was a brilliant explorer, navigator and cartographer who made three voyages to the Pacific Ocean, visiting 10 major island groups and more than 40 individual islands. He claimed the east coast of Australia for Britain, charted Newfoundland and New Zealand and was the first European to discover Hawaii (which he at the time named the Sandwich Islands). He also helped find a way of preventing scurvy, a disease that had killed huge numbers of sailors.

Because it's there...

When mountaineer George Mallory was asked why he wanted to climb Mount Everest, he said, '...because it's there." With such an attitude, mankind has taken on the biggest challenges of daring and endurance that nature offers.

North and South Poles

The South Pole was the first "extreme destination" to be tackled by explorers. The first five people to reach the Pole all belonged to a Norwegian party arriving on 14 December 1911, and led by Roald Amundsen. Thirty-three days later, Captain Robert Scott led a British

ABOVE Mount Everest, on the border of China and Nepal.

party to the same place. Tragically, Captain Scott and the other four members of his party all died on the return journey.

The first overland journey to the North Pole was made by the American Ralph Plaisted, reaching his goal on 19 April 1968.

Mount Everest
The first human beings to stand atop the world's highest point, Mount Everest, were the New Zealander Edmund Hillary and Nepalese Tenzing Norgay, who reached the summit on 29 May 1953. Three years later, a Swiss party reached the summit on 23–24 May, and various other climbers have replicated the feat since, though many have also perished in the attempt.

Swimming the Channel
Captain Matthew Webb of the United Kingdom was the first man to swim the English Channel when he completed the trip in 1875, taking 21 hours and 45 minutes. His spirit of adventure was to be his downfall though, when he died while trying to swim the Niagara River in 1883. The first woman to swim the Channel was an American, Gertrude Ederle, who took 14 hours, 31 minutes in 1926.

Around the world in 71 days

Name	Nationality	Date	Feat
Joshua Slocum	USA	1895–1898	First single-handed circumnavigation of the world.
Sir Francis Chichester	UK	1966–1967	First single-handed circumnavigation (one port of call).
Sir Robin Knox-Johnston	UK	1968–1969	First single-handed, nonstop circumnavigation.
Sir Chay Blyth	UK	1971	First westward, single-handed, nonstop circumnavigation.
Krystyna Chojnowska-Liskiewicz	Poland	1976–1978	First female single-handed circumnavigation.
Kay Cottee	Australia	1988	First woman to perform a solo nonstop circumnavigation.
Dame Ellen MacArthur	UK	2004–2005	Fastest single-handed (71 days, 14 hours) circumnavigation.

The Nobel Prize

Alfred Nobel, born in Sweden in 1833, amassed a vast fortune as the inventor of dynamite and owner of several companies and laboratories. On his death in 1896, he left his money for the establishment of the Nobel Prizes, which have been awarded since 1901 in recognition of outstanding human achievement. They were given for achievement in physics, chemistry, physiology or medicine, literature and peace. In 1968, a prize for economics was added. Each prize is worth around US$1.3 million and today

ABOVE Alfred Nobel.

they are arguably the most prestigious awards in the world. Since their foundation, prizes have been awarded to 758 people and 18 organisations.

Nobel Prize winners

The International Committee of the Red Cross has a won a record three times (for Peace), and its founder, Henry Dunant, won a prize himself in 1901. The UN High Commission for Refugees has won the Peace prize twice. The only other multiple winners are Marie

FACT

Only 46 women have won Nobel prizes, with 16 of those winning in the Peace category. Perhaps the two most famous winners are Mother Teresa of Calcutta and Marie Curie, a Polish scientist.

Curie (both for her work on radioactivity), Linus Pauling (1954 for Chemistry and 1962 for Peace), John Bardeen (1956 and 1972 for Physics) and Frederick Sanger (1958 and 1980 for Chemistry).

The youngest recipient of an award was Lawrence Bragg, who won the Physics prize in 1915 when he was just 25. At the other end of the scale, Raymond Davis, Jr was 87 when he won the Physics prize in 2002.

Only two people have voluntarily refused an award. Jean-Paul Sartre declined the Literature award in 1964, stating that it would compromise his integrity as a writer. Le Duc Tho turned down the Peace prize in 1973 on the basis that his country was not yet at peace.

Adolf Hitler was so infuriated the commitee nominated Carl von Ossietzky, a German journalist and peace activist imprisoned in a concentration camp, that he later forbade three German scientists – Richard Huhn, Adolf Butenandt and Gerhard Domagk – from accepting their prizes. The Russian writer Boris Pasternak refused the Literature prize in 1958 for fear of reprisals from the Soviet state.

In 1938, both Hitler and Mahatma Gandhi were considered for the Nobel Peace Prize, which finally went to Nansen International Office of Refugees. Gandhi was nomiated for the prize five times, but never won. However, in 1948, the year of Gandhi's death, no prize was given as the committee considered that there was "no suitable living candidate."

Alfred Nobel's will

It is said that Nobel's grand financial legacy was in part motivated by a premature obituary that was mistakenly published in a French newspaper, describing him as a "merchant of death." In any case, he was motivated to leave 94 per cent of his wealth to the Nobel Foundation, on which the prizes are drawn. The crucial lines in his will read:

The capital shall be invested by my executors in safe securities and shall constitute a fund, the interest on which shall be annually distributed in the form of prizes to those who, during the preceding year, shall have conferred the greatest benefit on mankind.

Olympic Games

The Olympic Games is perhaps the greatest sporting event in the world and the ultimate test for any athlete. The original Olympics were held in Ancient Greece, but the event was revived in 1896 by a French nobleman, Pierre Frèdy, Baron de Coubertin. Appropriately, the first modern games were held in Athens. They have occurred every four years since, with the exception of 1916, 1940 and 1944, when they were cancelled because of war. The Winter Games began in 1924. The Olympic Games are held in a different place every four years, with selection subject to fierce competition among cities hankering for international attention. London has hosted the modern Olympics three times, while Paris, Los Angeles, Lake Placid, Innsbruck, Athens and St. Moritz have hosted the Games twice. Tokyo will host its second Olympics in 2020.

The most recognisable symbol of the Olympic movement is the Olympic rings, featuring five intertwined rings representing the unity of five continents. They appear on a white background in red, blue, green, yellow and black, as every country has at least one of these colours in its flag.

Training an Olympic champion is no cheap business and over the history of the Games, the most successful countries have generally been rich. However, there are some notable exceptions – Ethiopia and Kenya in particular have produced more than their fair share of great middle- and long-distance runners.

FACT
In 1976, American swimmer Mark Spitz became the first athlete to win seven gold medals at a single Games. He won two more golds in his Olympic career.

Wonders of the world

The Seven Wonders of the ancient world

Traditionally, the Seven Wonders of the World were the marvels of classical civilisation described by Herodotus in the fifth century BCE – the list was later used and standardised by medieval writers.

Pyramids at Giza, Egypt *(c. 2600–2500 BCE) The pyramids are the oldest of the Seven Wonders, and the only to survive up until the present day. For four millennia, the Great Pyramid was the world's tallest structure.*

Hanging Gardens of Babylon *(sixth century BCE) A series of terraces on the banks of the Euphrates, built by Nebuchadnezzar II.*

Temple of Arthemis at Ephesus, Asia Minor (now Turkey) *(sixth century BCE) This marble temple was built in honour of the goddess of hunting and the Moon. After two centuries of degradation, it was rebuilt in the fourth century BCE, but destroyed by Goths in third century CE. A solitary column has been re-erected.*

Statue of Zeus at Olympia *(fifth century BCE) A 9-metre-high (30 foot) wooden statue of the Greek god Zeus covered with gold and ivory. It was destroyed by fire in 475 CE.*

Mausoleum at Halicarnassus, Asia Minor (now Bodrum, Turkey) *(fourth century BCE) The tomb of Mausolus at Halicarnassus was built by his widow. It was destroyed by an earthquake some time before the fifteenth century.*

Colossus of Rhodes *(305–292 BCE) A 32-metre-high (105 foot) bronze statue of the sun god Helios, this stood for less than a century. It was destroyed by an earthquake in 224 BCE.*

Pharos of Alexandria *(270 BCE) This was the world's first-known lighthouse, at the entrance of Alexandria harbour in Egypt. It once stood 122 metres (400 ft) high, but was in ruins by the fifteenth century.*

The seven wonders of the modern world

According to the American Society of Civil Engineers, the greatest civil engineering works of all time are the Empire State building (in New York), the Itaipú Dam (Brazil/Paraguay), the CN Tower (in Toronto, Canada), the Panama Canal, the Channel Tunnel (between France and Britain), the North Sea Protection Works (comprising the Zuider Zee Dam and the Oosterschelde Barrier in the Netherlands) and the Golden Gate Bridge (in San Francisco).

ABOVE The Golden Gate Bridge in San Francisco, California.

Glossary

agglomeration The action or process of collecting in a mass; a heap or cluster of often unrelated elements.

arbitration A process of settling an argument or disagreement in which the people or groups on both sides present their opinions and ideas to a third person or group.

biogenic Produced by living organisms.

biotic Of, relating to, or caused by living organisms.

cartographer A person who makes maps.

civilization The condition that exists when people have developed effective ways of organizing a society and care about art, science, etc.; a particular well-organized and developed society; all the societies of the world.

de facto A Latin term meaning "in reality" or "actually."

demography The statistical study of human populations especially with reference to size and density, distribution and vital statistics.

dialect A regional variety of language distinguished by features of vocabulary, grammar and pronunciation from other regional varieties and constituting together with them a single language.

estuary A water passage where the tide meets a river current; an arm of the sea at the lower end of a river.

immunity A condition of being able to resist a particular disease especially through preventing development of a pathogenic microorganism (like a virus or bacterium) or by counteracting the effects of its products.

infrastructure The basic equipment and structures (such as roads and bridges) that are needed for a country, region or organization to function properly.

inland Of, relating to or in the part of a country that is away from the coast or boundaries.

legitimacy The quality or state of being real, accepted, official or permissible by law.

linguistics The study of human speech including the units, nature, structure and modification of language.

literacy   The ability to read and write; knowledge that relates to a specific subject.

longevity   Length of life; the length of time that something or someone lasts or continues.

monotheistic   The doctrine or belief that there is only one true God.

prevalence   The degree to which something is common or widespread; the percentage of a population that is affected with a particular disease at a given time.

projection   An estimate of future possibilities based on a current trend.

republic   A government having a chief of state who is not a monarch and who in modern times is usually a president; a government in which supreme power resides in a body of citizens entitled to vote and is exercised by elected officers and representatives responsible to them and governing according to law; a political unit (as a nation) having such a form of government.

sovereign   One possessing or held to possess supreme political power; an acknowledged leader.

steppe   A large, flat area of land with grass and very few trees especially in eastern Europe and Asia.

terrain   A geographic area; a piece of land; the physical features of a tract of land.

xenophobia   Fear and hatred of strangers or foreigners or of anything that is strange or foreign.

For More Information

Centers for Disease Control and Prevention (CDC)
1600 Clifton Road
Atlanta, GA 30329-4027
800-CDC-INFO (800-232-4636)
Website: http://www.cdc.gov
The CDC works to protect America from health, safety and security threats, both foreign and in the US. Whether diseases start at home or abroad, are chronic or acute, curable or preventable, human error or deliberate attack, the CDC fights disease and supports communities and citizens to do the same.

International Monetary Fund
700 19th Street, NW
Washington, D.C. 20431
(202) 623-7000
Website: http://www.imf.org/external/index.htm
The IMF promotes international monetary cooperation and exchange rate stability, facilitates the balanced growth of international trade and provides resources to help members in balance of payment difficulties or to assist with poverty reduction. The IMF has 188 member countries.

National Geographic Society
1145 17th Street N.W.
Washington, D.C. 20036-4688
Website: http://www.nationalgeographic.com
The National Geographic Society has been inspiring people to care about the planet since 1888. It is one of the largest nonprofit scientific and educational institutions in the world. Its interests include geography, archaeology, natural science and the promotion of environmental and historical conservation.

Nature Conservancy
4245 North Fairfax Drive, Suite 100
Arlington, VA 22203-1606
(703) 841-5300
Web site: http://www.nature.org/?intc=nature.tnav
The mission of The Nature Conservancy is to conserve the lands and
waters on which all life depends.

United Nations Statistics Division
United Nations
New York, NY 10017
Website: http://unstats.un.org/unsd/default.htm
The Statistics Division is committed to the advancement of the
global statistical system. It compiles and disseminates global
statistical information, develops standards and norms for
statistical activities and supports countries' efforts to strengthen
their national statistical systems.

United Nations Visitors Centre
Department of Public Information
United Nations Headquarters
Room DHL-1B-154
New York, NY 10017
(212) 963-4475
Website: http://www.un.org/en
The United Nations is an international organization founded in 1945
after the Second World War by 51 countries committed to
maintaining international peace and security, developing
friendly relations among nations and promoting social progress,
better living standards and human rights.

The World Bank
1818 H Street, NW
Washington, DC 20433

(202) 473-1000
Website: http://www.worldbank.org
The World Bank is a vital source of financial and technical assistance
to developing countries around the world. It is not a bank in the
ordinary sense but a unique partnership to reduce poverty and
support development.

World Health Organization (WHO)
Avenue Appia 20 1211
Geneva 27
Switzerland
Tel.: + 41 22 791 21 11
Website: http://www.who.int/en
WHO is the directing and coordinating authority for health within
the United Nations system. It is responsible for providing
leadership on global health matters, shaping the health research
agenda, setting norms and standards, articulating evidence-based
policy options, providing technical support to countries and
monitoring and assessing health trends.

Websites

Because of the changing nature of Internet links, Rosen Publishing has
developed an online list of websites related to the subject of this book.
This site is updated regularly. Please use this link to access the list:

http://www.rosenlinks.com/GCM/World

For Further Reading

Brotton, Jerry. *Great Maps.* New York, NY: DK Smithsonian, 2014.

Brotton, Jerry. *A History of the World in 12 Maps.* New York, NY: Viking, 2013.

Daniels, Patricia S., et al. *National Geographic Almanac of World History,* Third Edition. Washington, DC: National Geographic, 2014.

Davis, Wade, et al. *Book of Peoples of the World.* Washington, DC: National Geographic, 2008.

DK Publishing. *The Economics Book: Big Ideas Simply Explained.* New York, NY: DK Adult, 2012.

DK Publishing. *Geography: A Visual Encyclopedia.* New York, NY: DK, 2013.

DK Publishing. *Knowledge Encyclopedia.* New York, NY: DK, 2013.

DK Publishing. *The Politics Book: Big Ideas Simply Explained.* New York, NY: DK Adult, 2013.

DK Publishing. *The Religions Book: Big Ideas Simply Explained.* New York, NY: DK Adult, 2013.

Griswold, Wendy. *Cultures and Societies in a Changing World (Sociology for a New Century).* Thousand Oaks, CA: SAGE Publications, 2012.

Harwood, Jeremy. *To the Ends of the Earth: 100 Maps that Changed the World.* Minneapolis, MN: Chartwell, 2012.

Hirschberg, Stuart, and Terry Hirschberg. *One World, Many Cultures,* Ninth Edition. Upper Saddle River, NJ: Longman, 2014.

Jennings, Ken. *Maphead: Charting the Wide, Weird World of Geography Wonks.* New York, NY: Scribner, 2012.

MacGregor, Neil. *A History of the World in 100 Objects.* New York, NY: Viking, 2011.

Miles, Jack, et al. *The Norton Anthology of World Religions* (2 vols.). New York, NY: W.W. Norton & Co., 2014.

Index

Picture credits

The publishers would like to thank the following for permission to reproduce images. Richard Burgess (illustrator): pp. 7, 20, 33, 49, 52, 60, 83, 93, 95, 108, 133; Science Photo Library: pp. 15, 34, 46, 111, 117; Getty Images: pp. 18, 101, 109, 119; UNESCO: p. 27; Per Christiansson: p. 13; Dr. Anthony R. Picciolo, NOAA: p. 22; Maps.com: pp. 16–17; Mike Lockhart, US Fish and Wildlife Service: p. 59; Howard Chandler Christy Papers, Special Collections, Skillman Library, Lafayette College: p. 92; Vitaly P. Sitnitsky at plakaty.ru: p. 92; Photolibrary.com: pp. 106, 140; Phil Scott: p.115; TheBo: p.120; NASA: pp. 121, 123, 124; UNESCO / Fayed: p. 130; Pavel Novak: p.134

Chart credits

The publishers would like to thank the following sources for information used in charts. *CIA World Factbook*, 2005: pp. 10, 11, 31, 37, 38, 39, 115; World Resources Institute and the Food and Agricultural Organization of the United Nations: p. 20; *The Cambridge Factfinder*, 2000: pp. 21; UNCLOS: p. 23; UN Statistics Division, 2002, p. 25; WHO: p. 41; World Resources Institute: p. 44; *Economist Pocket World in Figures*: pp. 51, 89, 96, 99, 126; Adherents.com: p. 54; United Nations: pp. 50, 86; *Ethnologue: Languages of the World*, 2005: p. 59; IMF: p. 94; *The Economist*: p. 96; Energy Information Administration, p. 103; International Labour Organization: p. 108; Forbes Billionaires List 2005: p. 110; Council on Tall Buildings and Urban Habitat: p. 114; *Top 10 of Everything*, 2005: p. 118; Airports Council International: p. 122